Additional Praise for
Reinventing the Entrepreneur

"*Reinventing the Entrepreneur: Turning Your Dream Business into a Reality* is not just an elegant roadmap of excellent business building skills . . . it's also a pathway to making them available to you—right here, right now. You'll be inspired by MaryEllen's teachings, and then get motivated to act and create a dream business of your own."

> —Kristi Frank, star of Season 1 of Donald Trump's *The Apprentice*, well-known for helping entrepreneurs start and grow their businesses

"MaryEllen Tribby, the consummate entrepreneur, has written a valuable book on how to start, run, and manage a successful small business. It teaches a clear, step-by-step process for growing your own business to seven and eight figure revenues."

> —Bob Bly, copywriter

"Entrepreneurs help meet our needs, fulfill our wants, and solve our problems. And they often get deservedly rich in the process. MaryEllen Tribby's excellent *Reinventing the Entrepreneur* is exactly the kind of practical, no-nonsense advice that can turn your own entrepreneurial dreams into reality. Highly recommended."

> —Alexander Green, author of *Beyond Wealth, The Secret of Shelter Island,* and *The Gone Fishin' Portfolio*

"MaryEllen's passion for helping people succeed always comes through in everything she does. The same is true with her book. For those who don't know or can't afford to spend time with MaryEllen, this book is the next best thing to having a personal one-on-one with her. It's as if she were there in front of you, revealing the secrets she's learned for success."

> —Sandy Franks, Publisher, Bonner and Partners

"MaryEllen Tribby takes you step by step through the process of turning your passions and expertise into a real money making business. Everything you need to know is laid out for you in this book. You will read it and then use it as resource guide as you realize your dream of creating and growing your own profitable business doing what you love."

> —David Lindahl, author, *Six Figure Second Income*

"Never before has anyone broken down the entire process from A to Z on how to start, build, and grow a successful online business with such simplicity. MaryEllen hits the nail on the head when she stresses the importance of building rapport and mutually beneficial relationships. This is truly a step-by-step book that any serious entrepreneur looking for consistent profit should have and refer to often."

—Vicki Irvin, CEO, Superwoman Lifestyle,
www.Superwomanlifestyle.com

"*Reinventing the Entrepreneur* proves once and for all that Mom knows best. MaryEllen Tribby, the hardest working mom on the planet, has written the ultimate roadmap for just about anyone who wants to start their own inbox magazine with a complete business model around it—soup to nuts . . . and no cooking required. Knowing MaryEllen's history and experience crushing it offline and then bringing a career of one success after another to the world of online marketing, there is no better person to write this blueprint. When your work is your play, life is most blissful . . . and *Reinventing the Entrepreneur* will give you all you need to make your dreams come true with a career that matches your core values and interests. It doesn't get better than that."

—Brian Kurtz, Executive Vice President, Boardroom Inc.

"Everyone touts their success online, and with the advent of *internet marketer metrics*, it is often difficult to distinguish real success from hydrogenated hyperbole. Does a 'Like' *really* translate into the bottom line? If so, what is the path to achieve that? How do you convert a person's clicks into income? In the 10-plus years I've known MaryEllen, she consistently brings practical, smart, and proven marketing ideas to bear in business. MaryEllen is a phenomenal marketer, a fantastic team builder, and her ability to deliver strong results so consistently is enduring."

—David Cross, direct marketer and organic farmer

"Once you're clear on your passions, the next step is discovering your dream career. MaryEllen Tribby has provided a roadmap for anyone who is committed to living a passionate life and making a great living at the same time."

—Janet Bray Attwood and Chris Attwood, co-authors of the
New York Times bestseller *The Passion Test—The Effortless Path to Discovering Your Life Purpose*

"This is the book that I wish was available when I first made the decision to start, build, and grow my online business. Not just filled with theory, MaryEllen has taken years of practical, real world experience and turned it into a step-by-step road map that anyone can follow to create a successful online presence. If you're looking to turn your passion into profit and leverage the power of the internet using a proven business model, then I highly recommend reading *Reinventing the Entrepreneur* by MaryEllen Tribby."

—Brian T. Edmondson, Publisher,
InternetIncomeCoach.com

"Today's 'we-centric' society no longer follows big, unattainable dreams. People today are interested in taking small actions to make their dreams a reality. MaryEllen Tribby's invigorating new book, *Reinventing the Entrepreneur,* is all about small actions and big results. If you are an entrepreneur who's serious about turning your dream business into reality, *Reinventing the Entrepreneur* gives you a nuts-and-bolts process to build that dream, one small step at a time."

—Michael Drew, co-author of *Pendulum: How Past Generations Shape Our Present and Predict Our Future*

"Trying to build a business without the fundamentals is like trying to build a home without a foundation. In *Reinventing the Entrepreneur,* MaryEllen Tribby teaches business fundamentals that can mean the difference between success and failure. Read this book, use it, and profit from it!"

—Noah St. John, inventor of Afformations and author of *The Book of Afformations*®

"Finally, a true step-by-step blueprint for turning your passion into a real business. I devoured it in one night! If you have dreams of running your own business (or want to grow your current one), then get this book today."

—Ryan Lee, entrepreneur, author, speaker, coach; ryanlee.com

"MaryEllen Tribby's *Reinventing the Entrepreneur: Turning Your Dream Business into a Reality* is a must read for anyone who is seeking to expand and shift their business mindset so the vision they have becomes their reality. In a changing world where the solo-preneur is being encouraged to become the conduit for ideas and innovations that are changing the face of how we do business, MaryEllen Tribby is a powerful force of inspiration who delivers her compelling wisdom, knowledge, and real-life success in a way that anyone can understand and most importantly, can use immediately. The successful entrepreneur can no longer stand for 'Business As Usual' and MaryEllen will show you why. Read this book now, or be left behind!"

—Paul Hoffman, Chief Creative and Inspiration Visionary, The Success Creation Institute

Reinventing the Entrepreneur

TURNING YOUR DREAM BUSINESS
INTO A REALITY

MaryEllen Tribby

Published by John Wiley & Sons, Inc., Hoboken, New Jersey.

Published simultaneously in Canada.

For general information on our other products and services or for technical support, please contact our Customer Care Department within the United States at (800) 762-2974, outside the United States at (317) 572-3993, or fax (317) 572-4002.

Wiley publishes in a variety of print and electronic formats and by print-on-demand. Some material included with standard print versions of this book may not be included in e-books or in print-on-demand. If this book refers to media such as a CD or DVD that is not included in the version you purchased, you may download this material at http://booksupport.wiley.com. For more information about Wiley products, visit www.wiley.com.

Library of Congress Cataloging-in-Publication Data:

Tribby, MaryEllen.
   Reinventing the entrepreneur : turning your dream business into a reality / MaryEllen Tribby.
      pages   cm
   Includes index.
   ISBN 978-1-118-58445-3 (cloth); ISBN 978-1-118-58447-7 (ePDF);
   ISBN 978-1-118-58458-3 (ePub)
      1. New business enterprises–Management.   2. Marketing research.
   3. Business planning.   I. Title.
   HD62.5.T75   2013
   658.1'1–dc23
                                                      2013016110

Printed in the United States of America.
10 9 8 7 6 5 4 3 2 1

This book is dedicated to the brave individuals who battled the unknown with no guarantees of success, who endured the heavy burden of failure constantly looming while relentlessly pursuing their dreams.

These individuals are known as ENTREPRENEURS.

To all of them who have followed their passion, embraced their purpose, who have honored their core values all the while working uncompromisingly to make the world a better place.

Contents

Part Two: Anatomy of Your Business

Part Three: The Useful and the Actionable

Part Four: The Art and Brilliance of a Community

Part Six: Big or Small, Your Choice

Acknowledgments

Writing a book never "just happens." It is a journey. One filled with intent, joy, frustration, commitment, compromise, inspiration, and, at times, isolation.

—MaryEllen Tribby

I would like to thank my family, starting with my husband, Patrick, who always puts my needs before his own. Next, my three precious children—Mikaela, my 14-year-old daughter, who inspires me to be a better person; Connor, my 12-year-old son, who has taught me the immense value of curiosity; and Delaine, my 8-year-old daughter, whose kindness brightens the day of everyone she encounters.

I would also like to thank my dear friends, colleagues, and mentors, from whom I have learned invaluable business and life lessons: Michael Masterson, Bill Bonner, Gary Goldstein, Joe Polish, Bill Glazer, Bob Bly, Tiffany Kennedy, Sir Richard Branson, David Cross, Chris Ruddy, James Malinchak, Julie McManus, Mike Koenigs, Ryan Lee, Jeff McDonald, Dr. Al Sears, Brian Tracy, Kristi Frank, Marie Forleo, Denise Gosnell, Jynell Berkshire, Noah St. John, Maria Andros, Jeff Walker, Craig Ballantyne, Michael Drew, Laura Betterly, Brian Edmondson, Dr. Susan Mathison, Deb Pilgrim, Roe Teed, Brian Johnson, Yanik Silver, Baeth Davis, Julia Kline, Lori Taylor, Ali Brown, Bill Harrison, Marci Shimoff, Catherine Astalos, Dave Lindahl, Clayton Makepeace, Wendy Makepeace, Jen Clement, Steven Bott, Rich Schefren, Dean Jackson, Shannon Allen, Teddy Garcia, Erica Rueschhoff, and to all of my Inbox Empire students all over the world, you nourish me!

I have a final thank you to Wallace Wang. Your insights and work ethic helped this book come to life!

Introduction: Turning Someday into Payday

The future belongs to those who believe in the beauty of their dreams.

—*Eleanor Roosevelt*

At this point we cannot rule out malignancy." Those were the doctor's exact words.

From that moment on, my life seemed like I was watching a silent movie. I felt my husband take my hand. I saw his mouth moving, asking the doctor a question. I saw the doctor's mouth move to answer my husband. I think this went on for some time.

But I'm not sure because I heard nothing. . . .

All I could think of were my three precious children.

My oldest was 10 years old at the time. I thought about all of our "girl" moments. I thought about the three breast cancer walks we had done together. I vividly recalled her questions about "walking in honor" of someone and why so many women had no hair, and explained what a "survivor" was. And I thought to myself, there would be no sugar coating this.

Quickly, my mind shifted to my son, only 8 years old at the time. I reflected on his love for baseball and how he relived each moment of his glory after each game. But I knew in his heart, he was a mama's boy. It made me reflect on all the beautiful Mother's Day cards he had made for me, all neatly kept in his scrapbook. I thought about what he would do in class next year while all the other kids were making cards for their moms. Would he sit in silence and make one for a mom that lived only in his heart?

Next, my thoughts were on my little princess, just 4 years old at the time. The happiest child I had ever had the privilege of knowing. I knew I had so little time with her. I deliberated whether I had made enough impact on her life that she would remember me at all. . . .

The next 20 days were pure hell.

I was poked, prodded, and sliced, and each evening my husband and I went through the many "what if" scenarios. However, on the 21st day, I was given the wonderful news that I did not have breast cancer.

After my husband and I celebrated in secret, my exuberance soon turned to sorrow. It was the most paradoxical moment of my life. I had just been given back my life, yet I was dismayed.

You see, two years prior to my breast cancer threat, I had bought and registered the domain WorkingMomsOnly.com.

I did so because many women were constantly asking me how I "did it all." How could I be a big-time CEO and run a huge publishing company, write a best-selling book, speak about business and marketing all over the world, and still have a loving marriage with three wonderful kids?

I knew that someday I would start and run a business to help other working moms fulfill their dreams and live the life they deserved. And that was the reason for my dismay: I had said "someday" far too often.

Even though I had a job I treasured, I was not living my true calling. I was not reaching out to help transform and lead the working moms' community. I knew that this was the community that had more responsibilities than any other single group of people. I knew that this was the group of people that had more influence on the future of our country. And I knew that I was the person who had to do it.

The next day, during the worst unemployment our country had seen since the Great Depression, the worst housing market in history, and a dismal stock market, I resigned from a job where I earned more than 16 times the average American household income.

And I have never looked back.

Maybe you, too, have a dream of starting your own business but just aren't sure how to start.

That's okay because I'm going to help you. I'll walk you through what I believe is the best online business model in the world.

Here's the best part. Your business can be anything. I had a dream of helping working moms and building my business around that. You can build your dream business around almost any niche with this business model.

You just need to do it—let's get started.

PART

THE WHO AND THE WHY

One's work usually occupies more than half of one's waking life. Choosing work that does not bring happiness will lead to a life that is mostly disappointing.

—*Bo Bennett*

CHAPTER

1

Idea Brainstorming: Fun, Fast, and Easy

Everyone has plenty of ideas. In fact, you may have a great idea right now that you're itching to get started on, but wait! The real problem isn't coming up with a great idea, but recognizing when you have a good one. All it takes is one good idea and you can make a fortune.

So how do you know when you have that one good idea? First, you come up with lots of ideas and sift through them to find the best one. That's the first part behind idea brainstorming.

To help get you started, answer the following questions:

1. What are my hobbies and interests?
2. What are some of my life experiences and achievements?
3. What problems, big or small, have I solved in my life?

You may be thinking, "Gosh, that's cute, that's quaint. I would love nothing more than to have hobbies and interests, but I work so hard that I don't have time for any of that." So let me ask you, "What would you like to do if you did have more time?"

Maybe you don't get to do them right now, but don't limit yourself. You might be saying, "I would love to have my own business, and one of my favorite hobbies is kites. I love flying and building kites, and I would love to teach others how to do the same. I would love to do an inbox magazine on everything about kites. But who would want that?" Well, the answer is plenty of people. Did you know that hundreds of thousands of people search on the term *building kites* each month? So put down every idea to start. Later, I'll tell exactly how you can determine whether your idea might make a good business.

When you think about your life experiences and achievements, don't overlook anything, no matter how simple or obvious you think it might be. Did you raise children, start a business, stay married for 50 years, plan your own wedding, learn a complicated software program, home-school your kids, or fly airplanes?

Whatever you did, that's something someone else would want to know about, so put that down, too. These are all good life experiences and achievements. You don't have to have climbed Mount Everest. Just think about the little victories in life. I knew a student who started a business that literally explained how to get your child into an Ivy League school. She had gone through every step from teaching the right way to study for the SAT test to preparing for the in-person interviews. Because she had already gone through that process, she wrote her first special report and sold it online. Later, she turned her idea into a working business.

Now think about some significant problems you might have solved in your life. Did you lose weight, help a loved one through an illness, find a great job, rebuild your home after a natural disaster, survive bankruptcy, or start over after divorce? Maybe you just know how to solve seemingly minor problems like getting rid of rodents from your house or garden. There may be some painful memories, but those areas in life where people feel the most distressed is where you can make the most money. Plus, you can help the most people by doing the most good.

Many people have been beaten down by life, so they may feel negative and say, "What? Are you kidding me? I don't have time for hobbies and interests. Life experience? Achievements? I haven't been able to do anything, and that's why I'm so frustrated. Problems big or small? I've got problems but I haven't solved them."

I knew a woman who kept resisting the idea of writing down her hobbies or achievements. Finally, I asked her, "Who is someone in your life that you really respect? Somebody in your life that you truly admire and love?" After much thinking, she finally told me about her friend, Cindy.

Then I said, "Okay, tell me something about Cindy. What are her hobbies and her interests? What are some of Cindy's life experiences and achievements? And what problems big or small has Cindy solved?"

Suddenly, this lady started going through this exercise by thinking about other people in her life. Just by going through this exercise, she soon realized that ideas are limitless.

While you may not always like to give your friends credit, you probably know some pretty smart people. You might know somebody who is a really good salesperson, realtor, or mortgage broker who has survived this most recent downturn and are still making money despite all that.

Maybe you know someone who got divorced or lost 100 pounds. What process did they go through, and what is their life like now? As a matter of fact, most people have already forgotten great ideas until they make a conscious effort to recall them.

Ultimately, every business is about someone else, so it doesn't always have to be about you. When this lady started thinking about her friend, Cindy, she started thinking, "You know what? I've done something like that as well!"

So try to get out of your own head and think of someone else because that can get you thinking a lot bigger. Pretty soon, you will have several ideas to choose from.

Discover the Three "P's": Passion, Purpose, and Profits

Whatever idea you come up with, make sure it's something that you are truly interested in and passionate about. Tap into your inner calling. Don't just chase the money. When I started WorkingMomsOnly.com, I didn't do it just for the money but because I wanted to teach other working moms how to have a healthier, wealthier, more blended lifestyle. It is my firm belief that working moms have more responsibility than any other single group of people and that they have more influence as well. I knew this was a market I had to serve. That's why it's such a pleasure and an easy business for me.

If you're really excited and passionate about something, running your business will be a breeze. Not only will it be easy, but it will be a lot more fun as well. When you marry your passion and your purpose, the profits will follow.

Remember, you're never limited to just one idea. You can eventually have your own empire, so don't feel that where you start today is necessarily where you are going to finish. If you have several great ideas, start with the one you are most passionate about, the one that defines your purpose. If you are still stuck, add the experience factor into the equation. Another reason why it was easy for me to start WorkingMomsOnly.com was that I was a working mom for 11 years, with multiple children. I had experience and knew I could help others.

For some additional ways to jog your brain for ideas, go to magazine sites on the Internet. If there's a particular market you're thinking about and it has its own magazine, then it's probably big enough for an inbox magazine. If the market is big enough to justify its own association, then it's probably a big enough market for you to go after.

Go directly to Amazon.com/magazines, or just go to Amazon and look for the search box in the left-hand column (see Figure 1.1). Look where it says magazine subscriptions, where it lists featured categories such as automotive, photography, brides and

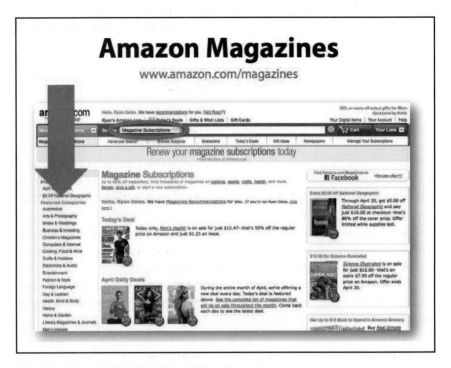

Figure 1.1   Browse through Amazon.com's list of magazines.

wedding, business and investing, children's magazines, computer and Internet, cooking, food, wine, and crafts. You will see endless categories.

If you're thinking you don't have any hobbies, scan through that list. I'd be willing to bet that you find something in there that interests you. Look at any magazines you may subscribe to or that catch your eye on the newsstand. Obviously, you have some interests and hobbies, so browsing through magazines can be a great way to jog your imagination.

To browse through another list of magazines, go to Magazines .com and click the Browse tab. Now you can see all the most popular magazine categories such as Fashion, Health & Fitness, or Sports.

Besides scanning for magazine topics, look at the magazine headlines. Essentially, every cover story is a headline designed to grab your attention. Look at a men's magazine like *Men's Health* or *GQ* and you'll notice which topics are hot and how they grab your attention by the way they're written. Magazines have a big job. They have to grab the eye of someone walking by a newsstand; so don't forget to look at those cover stories and topics for ideas.

Here's a list of magazine sites to browse through in addition to browsing through your local newsstand:

- www.Amazon.com/magazines
- www.Magazines.com
- www.MagsDirect.com
- www.MrMagazines.com

Right now, I want you thinking in terms of market selection. Magazines.com is another great source. Just click on the Browse tab and you'll see so many different markets and groups that you can go after (see Figure 1.2).

Magazines.com is favorite source, especially if you want to focus more on business-to-business opportunities. As long as there's a magazine or a trade journal for a particular market, it's big enough to justify going into that field. If there happens to be an association for that field, then it's definitely going to be big enough. Here are two ways to find directories of associations:

- www.MarketingSource.com/associations
- www.weddles.com/associations (FREE!!)

Figure 1.2   Another source of magazines is Magazines.com.

There's an association for practically anything—from agriculture to astronomy, automotive, career counseling, building real estate, or chemistry. Weddles happens to be free, although you can try MarketingSource.com if you're willing to pay for information. Generally, I would stick with the free directory.

Is It Sellable?

When you think you have an idea of what you want to do, the next (and most important) step is to determine how sellable that idea might be. When I started WorkingMomsOnly.com, I knew it had to be a sellable idea. If it wasn't, then it could have been my hobby, but it would not have been my business. So when I say "sellable," I mean you will make money with this idea!

Use the following list to identify a sellable idea. The more categories you can check off for that idea, the more sellable that idea will be. Generally, the most sellable ideas are those that help others solve a problem fast such as making money or losing weight. I like to call these Big Money Categories (see Figure 1.3).

"Big Money" Categories

☐ Make money

☐ Save money

☐ Look good

☐ Improve health/longevity

☐ Increase popularity

☐ Increase security

☐ Give inner peace

☐ Increase free time

☐ Have more fun

Figure 1.3   Identifying a sellable idea.

When solidifying your idea, make sure that you can check off at least two of these boxes. You'll know that you've found a sellable idea when you can check off multiple categories for what you want to deliver.

For example, when I look at WorkingMomsOnly.com, I know I can check off make money, save money, look good, improve health, increase popularity, increase security, give inner peace, increase free time, and have more fun. When you are talking about a lifestyle, you pretty much have all of these categories covered.

Of course, don't feel like you have to check them all off. If you've got an inbox magazine on yoga, you might check off only look good, improve health, and give inner peace.

If you've got an idea on productivity, you might check off only make money, save money, increase free time, and have more fun.

Even if you can check off only make money, then you probably have a winner because everyone wants to make more money. That's a hot spot that people will pay money to learn. People will always pay money to learn how to make money, save money, and look good.

They'll also pay money for their health, pride, popularity, and personal development like inner peace, security, and free time. Don't forget about those hobbies. Hobby sites are so popular because almost everyone wants to have more fun. So that's one you will always be able to check off with a hobby-related idea.

Quick Start Summary

Remember, your idea should meet these criteria:

- You must be passionate about the idea.
- There must already be an existing market for your idea.
- The idea must be sellable.

Once you have an idea that meets all three criteria, you can move on to thinking about markets versus topics, which you'll learn about in the next chapter.

Step 1: Take out a piece of paper or open up your laptop and write three ideas that you have always wanted to do as a business. At this point, it does not matter how outrageous they may sound. You just want to start putting down your ideas.

Step 2: See who else is selling the same thing in your market. Remember, it is a good thing to have competition. Being the first one into a market is usually not what you want. If you have several companies selling the same thing to the same market, it means your idea is a sellable one.

Step 3: Pick the best idea out of the three. If all of the above criteria are equal, select the idea that you are most passionate about. Remember, you need to get started; once you have your first inbox magazine up and running, you can always come back to your other ideas.

2

Markets versus Topics: Understand the Difference and Prosper

Now that you have your idea, you need to understand the difference between markets and topics. A market is who you are selling to, which is a community of like-minded people. A topic is what you are delivering, which is the subject matter of your content. With Working Moms Only, the market is clearly working moms, although there are also working dads and working women who don't have kids. However, my advocacy is for working moms. This is the group of people I have chosen to serve. This is when my passion and purpose and profits come together.

In terms of your topic, the what, the topics can be anything. There are inbox magazines that cater strictly to foreign exchange (forex) traders. That's their market, their who. Yet the topics published in an inbox magazine to these forex traders range from forex trading to how to build your own solar panels. That's because your topics cover the interests of your market. Many forex traders are also interested in solar panels—how to use them and how to build them—so there's a lot of crossover, even though the topic of solar panels has nothing to do with forex trading. Topics on WorkingMomsOnly.com range from how to be the superstar in your company to how to raise compassionate kids.

Another great example is an inbox magazine called Daily Wealth. As the name implies, this inbox magazine's primary focus is on investing. They offer advice and opinions on stocks, gold, exchange-traded funds, and more, but they have had many actual issues such as "how to make your own natural cleaning products" to "this powerful vitamin is for more than just colds."

That's because they not only understand the demographic of their readers but the psychographic as well. They understand that this subject matter is important to many of their readers, who are contrarians. Such readers want their advice from a trusted source.

That is why you can see that the most important question to ask is: Who's my market? You could have the greatest topic but you'll need to present it differently for different markets. Your market shapes the topic.

For example, suppose your topic is patient referral strategies. Now if your market consists of dentists, you'll need to present that topic to cater to the problems and needs of dentists. Take that same topic of patient referral strategies and present it to chiropractors and you'll need to adapt the topic to meet the needs of chiropractors. If you just present the same topic to both dentists and chiropractors, you won't meet the unique needs of either one.

If Working Moms Only offers an article about time management, it's specifically directed toward working mothers even though that same information could be useful for golfers, doctors, or accountants. If you don't know, understand, and relate to your market, your topics can't help them.

Your topic might be marathon training, but you'll present it one way to one market of long-distance runners and a second way to a market of just female long-distance runners. Don't be general—pick a market.

If your topic is how to survive a divorce, you'll definitely need to adapt that information depending on whether your market is men or women. If your topic is about offering dating advice, you'll have different information when targeting singles under 30 than if you were targeting widows and widowers. What if your market were video game players? Then your dating advice would need to meet their specific needs to be useful.

Your market doesn't limit what topics you can offer, but it does help you sharpen each topic to specifically meet the needs of your target audience. If your inbox magazine catered to video game enthusiasts, you could promote video game products along with back pain products (since many of these guys sit in a chair all day long) and dating advice for (mostly) guys who are introverts.

You've got to shift your mind-set from just focusing on topics to focusing on markets. If you picture a specific market in your head and stay true to that market, you'll deliver content that uniquely meets the needs of that target audience. Working moms might want to know about cloth diapers and organic laundry detergent, but they may also want to know about starting their own business and exercise as well.

I knew a woman who created an entire business around surviving a divorce for women. Her topics expanded from just surviving a divorce as a woman to how divorced women could get a date and how to deal with their relationship with their children.

By becoming an advocate for a particular market, you can talk about multiple topics. As the people in your market grow, you can grow and mature with them. If you're too narrowly focused on your topic, such as how to survive a divorce and only how to survive a divorce, guess what? You may have the greatest information in the world, but once they read it, they're done with you.

Now if you're the person who advocates for them, you can show them how to survive a divorce. Then after they've gotten past that, you can show them how to date and maintain a relationship after a divorce. Then you can teach them a seemingly unrelated but still useful topic such as how to manage money as a divorced parent.

That's why a market is so much more important than a topic. Think market. If you try to reach everyone at once, you'll wind up reaching no one. Only after you choose a target market can you later scale out and reach other qualified people. With Working Moms Only, the market is working moms, but other qualified people include working dads, single women, and married women who don't have kids, but they are not the target market.

So you need to identify your target market and your qualified market. That shows you your total available market. Then there's your potential market, which consists of people who aren't in your market just yet, but may one day get there. So Working Moms Only's breakdown of markets might look like this:

- Target market: Working moms
- Qualified market: Working fathers, single women, married women without kids
- Potential market: Teenagers, grandparents

If you didn't know your market, you could waste a lot of time and money trying to reach everyone. If you shoot for the general population as your target market, you're going to find it much harder to make any money.

Starting Small Is Better

One of the best case studies I can share with you is Facebook.

Facebook grew by following these exact same principles. When Facebook first got started, it was only for students of Harvard. Then it grew and expanded to include students who were attending any Ivy League school. Then it expanded to all colleges. From colleges, it went to all types of students including high school. Finally, it expanded to the general population (see Figure 2.1).

This is how you build your inbox magazine business. Start small and keep getting bigger and bigger. You can't market to everybody unless you're a big company with a multimillion-dollar advertising budget. Your business is never for everyone. Your business is only for the most qualified people who are most likely to pay you money.

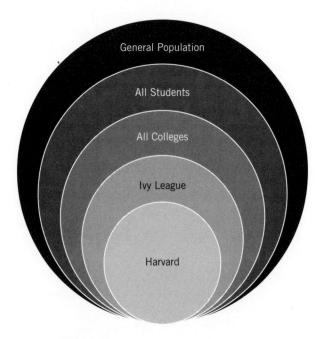

Figure 2.1   The growth of Facebook.

Trying to reach and market to everyone is simply a waste of time and money.

Do you know how Nike got its start? In track programs. Gatorade got started by marketing a sports drink to athletes at the University of Florida. Almost every big, national brand today started small and grew organically.

If you want to find out if you have a good market, ask yourself this question: does my market self-identify?

How can you tell if a market self-identifies? Look to see if there are magazines that cater to them, clubs, associations, trade shows, membership sites, support groups, or forums. Do people refer to themselves as something? Do they tell themselves, "I'm a golfer, I'm a working mom, or I'm a kite-building enthusiast?"

If you can find a magazine, a club, an association, a trade show, a membership site, a support group, or a forum, you're on the right track. If you can't find any of those things, I would proceed with caution. Maybe you're thinking a little too small. Maybe you need to pull back a little or go in a different direction.

Find your market first. Then find the topics that would satisfy your market.

CHAPTER

3

Determining Market Size: Easy as the Three Bears—It's Got to Be Just Right

Once you have your idea, know the difference between markets and topics, and have isolated your target market, it's time to figure out the size of your market. If the market is too big, you'll spread your energy trying to reach too many people. If the market is too small, it won't be profitable.

To determine a market's size, you can use three free sources and one paid source:

- Google (free)
- Wikipedia (free)
- Yahoo! Answers/WikiAnswers (free)
- Uclue.com (paid)

To use Google, type in "number of" followed by the name of your market such as "working moms" or "forex traders." For example, suppose you wanted to know the market of marathon runners. Visit Google and search for "number of marathoners." This will display a list of links.

Click on the links that seem most relevant, such as Marathon Guide, which offers its 2007 USA marathon report. This will show you that the total number of marathon finishers in 2007 was 407,000 people. More important, the growth curve shows a slight dip in marathon finishers in 2001, but from 2002 on, the market keeps steadily growing. By 2007, there were over 400,000 marathon finishers (see Figure 3.1).

Remember, these are people who actually finished marathons, but there are many more people who are just marathon enthusiasts. By using these rough numbers, you can determine the approximate size of your market.

Also notice the breakdown of male and female marathon finishers. If you happen to offer marathon training for women, you've got your number right there.

This is known as keyword research, which Wikipedia defines as a practice used by search engine optimization professionals to find and research actual research terms people enter.

Such keyword research will tell you what people are interested in, and in what relative numbers. Better yet, it reveals the *actual language* people are using when they think about those topics, which provides you with better insight on how to speak their language.

You don't have to be a computer professional to master this. You simply type keywords into Google and look at the number of

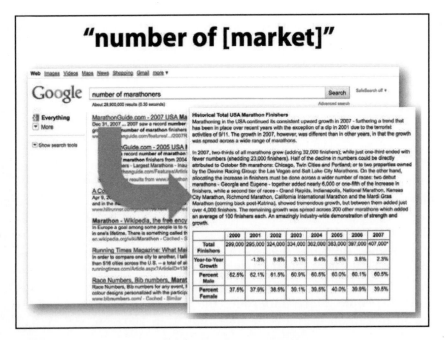

Figure 3.1   Using Google to determine the market size of marathoners.

searches. If less than 10,000 people per month are searching for that particular topic, there's probably not enough people in that market. If you've got millions, then you might want to niche it down a little bit more to find a less crowded market.

Where's There's a Good Question, There's a Great Answer

Wikipedia.org is another source of great information. Answers.com is a question-and-answer site where you can ask a question and wait for others to answer you, sometimes for free or sometimes for a small fee. Often, the questions that I wanted answered had already been asked and answered. Before Answers.com allows you to ask a question, they want you to search if it has already been asked and answered. Yahoo! Answers (answers.yahoo.com) works the same way.

Another question-and-answer site is Uclue, which actually has paid researchers including graduate students, professors, and other people with a lot of knowledge and time on their hands. You'll have to pay for the answers, but the amount of research that they will do in exchange for a relatively small amount of money is pretty amazing.

When searching for information on Uclue.com, ask for market size in two ways:

- Total revenue generated. (What are these people spending in a year?)
- Total number of potential customers.

Since you're paying for answers in Uclue.com, avoid long, multipart questions. Don't ask 15 different questions when you really just want to know the market size.

Check the category for pricing ideas prior to bidding. When you go into a particular category, you can ask, "Hey, I want somebody to research for me this information and I'm willing to pay $50." If everybody in that category is offering $50, then you can offer $50 or $60 and you'll get a response.

For categories related to the health, engineering, or medical field, the researchers typically command higher pay, so you'll have to bid more for that information. A typical bid might range from $50 to $100, but check your category for what is normal first.

Let's say you wanted to do an inbox magazine for cat owners because you just love cats. You might be trying to sell cat urine remover or odor stain remover, so you would be interested to hear what cat owners spend on that. So you might ask Uclue.com, "What's the total number of cat owners in the United States, and how much money do cat owners spend to remove cat urine odors and stains each year?"

Remember, we want to get the market size in two ways: How big is the market? How many potential customers?

Don't isolate your questions just to cat urine odor and stains. Just ask, "How much money do people in the United States spend on their cats on average?"

In this particular example, we asked this question and got an answer within a few days at a cost of $75. This included the sources where they found this information so you could verify it for yourself. If you want information from professional market research companies such as Forrester.com, Hoovers.com, or Gartner.com, you'll generally pay more for these reports.

A good rule of thumb is to target a single-digit market share such as 3 to 5 percent. In the marathon example, there were 400,000 finishers. If 400,000 people finish, there might be at least a million people interested in running a marathon. Imagine getting 3 to 5 percent of all those people as free subscribers to an inbox magazine. Just targeting marathon finishers alone would reach 12,000 to 20,000 people.

Many people think, "Oh, I'm going to get a 20 percent market share." That usually doesn't happen, but a 3 to 5 percent market share is completely possible. Imagine having just 5 percent of working moms in the world. That number is gigantic.

To start thinking about a market, you need around 400,000 to 500,000 people to turn it into a business. Just remember, you also need to be passionate about it as well!

If 3 to 5 percent of the market doesn't seem to have enough people, you may need to broaden your market. Rather than focus on marathon running, perhaps focus on long-distance running.

Another market research tool is Standard Rate and Data Services (SRDS), which compiles the subscriber size of most magazines. So if you look at the SRDS for a golf magazine, you might find that they have approximately three million subscribers. That's enough to let you know if your topic has a big enough market.

Remember, you don't just need the right market, but you also need to narrow your focus toward the right niche. Don't try to reach everybody. If you target too broad a market, you'll wind up reaching everyone but appealing to no one.

Start small. Remember the story of Facebook starting out just for Harvard graduates and broadening their base from there. By targeting a niche and meeting their unique needs, you'll get your inbox magazine business started off reaching the types of potential customers who will want what you have to offer.

4

Your Subscriber Avatar: Knowing Your Ideal Customer

After you've selected your market, know that it's big enough, and looks like it will be a lot of fun as a great hobby or lifestyle business, the next step is to create one, two, or even three subscriber avatars. A subscriber avatar defines the customer who embodies the most common characteristics of the market you're targeting. In other words, who is your *who*?

First, pick a name that makes the most sense to you. You don't need a last name, but you need to give your average customer, the person that you're thinking about, a name. Now when you're considering creating a product, writing copy, or writing an issue, you can ask yourself, "Is Julie going to be interested in this? Is Ron going to find this useful? Is Ben going to be able to act on my advice?" You actually want to think along those lines.

Remember, you're not just building a list of names and e-mail addresses. You're building a community of like-minded people who are going through the same challenges or have the same experiences, interests, and hobbies. Ultimately, they are looking to you for help. When you identify with a single person, you'll write to someone specific so your end result will be better and more distinct.

You might actually have more than one customer avatar to represent both men and women on your list and in your community. If that's the case, you want to make sure that you deliver a message that resonates with both of them.

However, most markets will be ultra-specific with common demographics. For example, suppose you have an inbox magazine targeting financial investors. Would you have women on your investor list? Of course you would. Would you have a customer avatar for women? No, because you don't need one. The majority of investors are men. A typical customer avatar might be a man named Ron who is 58 years old, married, conservative, with an annual income of $95,000 and above. His children are grown and out of the house. Now he has more time to spend trying to improve his financial portfolio.

By specifying your typical customer in detail (see Figure 4.1), you make it easy to focus your business to meet your subscriber avatar's needs.

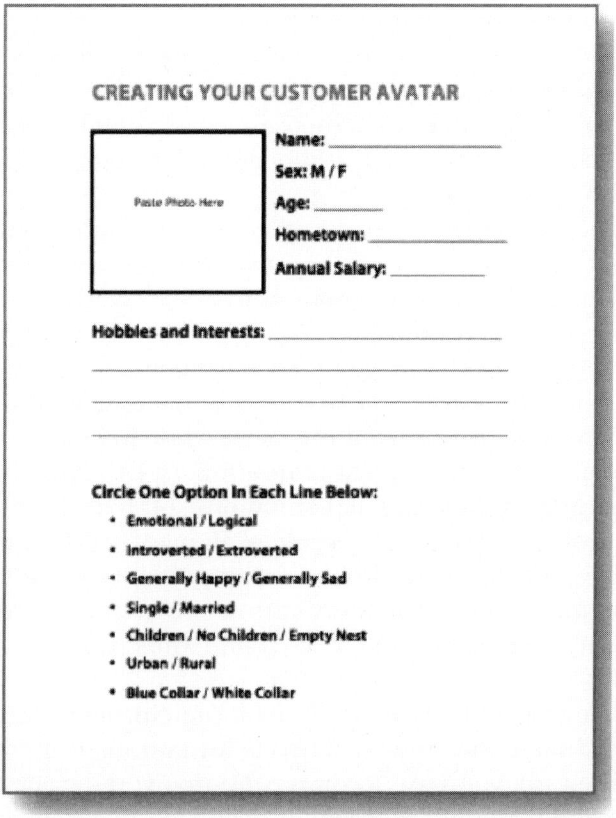

CREATING YOUR CUSTOMER AVATAR

Paste Photo Here

Name: _____

Sex: M / F

Age: _____

Hometown: _____

Annual Salary: _____

Hobbies and Interests: _____

_____

_____

_____

Circle One Option In Each Line Below:

- Emotional / Logical
- Introverted / Extroverted
- Generally Happy / Generally Sad
- Single / Married
- Children / No Children / Empty Nest
- Urban / Rural
- Blue Collar / White Collar

Figure 4.1   Creating a subscriber avatar.

Give your avatar a name and decide on their sex—male or female? What's their age? Are they 58 or 27? Where do they live? What's their hometown? What's their annual salary? You can get some of this information from your market research. What are some of their other hobbies and interests? Think like a fiction writer turned detective.

In an interview with J. K. Rowling, she explained how before she ever wrote the very first Harry Potter book, she already knew everybody's backstory. She knew where they lived and their hopes, dreams, and fears because she wanted them to feel complete. She wanted you to believe they were real human beings.

Just as you are a complex person, so are your customers. When you think about who your customers are, you can discover their other interests. For example, forex traders are mostly older, conservative, and wealthy men, and many of them are interested in urban survival. They may want to know how to make their own bomb shelters and grow and harvest their own food supply. Knowing this, you can offer them those types of products that meet their interests. When you start talking to your customers, you'll begin to hear their other similar interests, and then you can update your customer avatar.

Your customer avatar will always evolve. While heading up large financial publishing companies, I discovered that the biggest hobby for people interested in the financial markets is gardening. Who would have thought? I learned this only because I talked to these customers and asked for feedback. I sent them surveys and I kept asking them, "What do you do on your vacation?" and "Where did you spend your time?" The most common answer I kept getting from both questions was, "I spend my time in the garden." Just knowing that opened up a whole new universe to go out and find new customers.

This can add a whole new dimension to your inbox magazine. You can say something like, "Hey, this is going to sound a little bit weird, but I love gardening and I know most of you do, too, so I wanted you to meet one of my favorite gardening experts. If you think it's boring, let me know. If you like him, let me know. I just want to give you a full experience and tell you what I'm all about."

Your subscribers will probably love it, so your inbox magazine doesn't always have to stay on topic. Yes, you'll have some people who may question this information and tell you, "This isn't about trading or investing."

Maybe they get upset and go away, but most people may be pleasantly surprised at something new and different once in a while, so try this out. Remember, you do not want to swim in a sea of sameness.

Birds of a Feather Flock Together

To identify the hometown of your subscriber avatar, go to Google and search for "Google trends" or just visit www.google.com/trends (see Figure 4.2).

Now type in your market name or primary interests. Let's say you want to do an inbox magazine for sugar gliders, which are a kind of rat with wings. For some reason, people keep them as pets.

Go to Google trends, type in "sugar gliders," and you'll see the cities that searched the most for sugar gliders such as Salt Lake City,

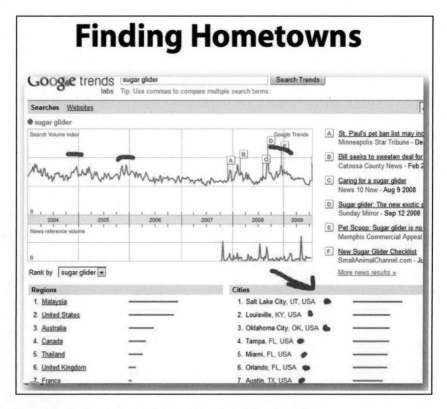

Figure 4.2   Finding your subscriber hometown through Google trends.

Louisville, Oklahoma City, Tampa, Miami, Orlando, and Austin, Texas.

While these cities may seem random, if you look closer, you'll notice that these are all mostly college towns. Now you can get an even more complete picture of your subscriber avatar besides a name and age. Remember, I've already given my avatar a name and an age. Now I know their typical city.

Now go back to Google and search for pictures of your typical person. For example, you might say, "My prospective subscriber is Ashley. She's 18 years old and lives in Salt Lake City." Search Google for 18-year-old women named Ashley in Salt Lake City and you'll likely find several pictures. Find the one you like, print it out, and now you have a face so you can look at your subscriber avatar.

By actually putting a face to your avatar's description, you can ask more emotional questions about that person. Are they generally happy or sad? Single or married? Children, no children, or empty nest? Urban or rural? Blue collar or white collar?

At Working Moms Only, my typical avatar is a married working mom. She has three kids and is 43 years old. Her biggest challenge is wanting to make more money while spending more time with her kids. She is also trying to stay fit and have a better relationship with her spouse.

Now don't get me wrong, I have plenty of single moms on my list. I also have many men as well. But we are talking about the typical subscriber.

Once you know the basic emotional background of your avatar, you can easily project different life circumstances onto your list. For example, if you're happy and married, you can ask people on your list, "Isn't it crazy when your husband does this and that?"

Now if you were focusing on traders, you would need to keep your communication with them more logical, since that's the way most of them think. Also many traders are also more introverted, single, white collar, and empty nesters. Knowing this, you can select stories that will resonate with most people on your list. Nothing will appeal to everyone, but you want to reach the majority of your subscribers.

Your subscriber avatar helps keep you focused on who you want and need to reach. For your own inbox magazine, create that first subscriber avatar. You may eventually need more avatars, but you always need to start with one avatar that represents your main market.

The time to create more than one avatar is when you expand your market.

When you're targeting your first 1,000 subscribers, you should have a clear idea who your main market is by creating an avatar that represents those typical subscribers. When you start expanding your subscriber base, that's the time to update and create multiple avatars. Facebook, Nike, and Gatorade all started by targeting a single market first. Only after they started to grow and reach out to slightly different markets did they need to update and create multiple avatars.

So your action item at this point is to create your first customer avatar. Copy the avatar form, fill it up, and post that description and picture right by your computer. When you're publishing your inbox magazine, you want to read it. Don't read it through your own eyes, but read it through the eyes of that customer avatar that you just created. When you're selecting offers, ask yourself, would Ron like this? Would Ashley like this? Always ask that question. As long as you have your avatar right in front of your face, you won't forget about him or her.

When I started Working Moms Only, I started with one customer avatar. As Working Moms Only grew, people sent pictures of themselves and their kids. Now I use those pictures, along with my avatar, to help me stay focused on my subscribers.

As you meet people at events, conferences, and trade shows, take lots of pictures. Now your picture of the people on your list gets fuller, more real, and more intimate, and you'll get better at knowing exactly what information your list will love to see next.

CHAPTER

5

Competitive Analysis: The Direct and Indirect

Competitive analysis is about knowing your competition. One of the fastest, easiest, and cheapest ways to learn more about your competition is by searching for them on Google.

Not only will Google help you discover if there are other inbox magazines out there covering the same topic, but Google can also help you uncover any forums or other online communities that reach your main target market.

First of all, don't think of competition as something bad that can discourage you from starting your own inbox magazine. Instead, think of competition as a way to verify that your market can be lucrative and as a way to see what works. You want to see what your competitors are doing right so you can mimic that. You also want to see what your competitors might be missing so you can fill that need.

Two Is Better Than One

Basically, you want to identify two categories of competition: direct and indirect competitors.

A direct competitor is someone selling the same thing to the same market in the same way as you. If you're marketing an inbox magazine targeted at folks with back pain and somebody else also offers an inbox magazine targeted at folks with back pain and they're selling the exact same thing to the exact same market in the exact same way, that's a direct competitor.

If somebody is a direct competitor, don't look at him or her as a threat. Think of them as a possible panelist for your inbox magazine, or even a possible partner in a joint venture. Don't ever be the person who says, "I don't want to have anything to do with that company because they're selling something similar."

One of the reasons why Agora is such an enormously successful company is the cooperation and cross-promotion among the different companies within Agora. There are approximately 25 financial publishing companies inside of Agora. Since they're all pretty much selling the same information, they're direct competitors of each other, yet they all cooperate. They're panelists and joint venture partners for one another. That's the way that you should be thinking about competitors, too.

If you've selected the right market, then the people in that market will be passionate and enthusiastic about it. They're not just going to subscribe to just one source. People who are passionate and excited about golf might subscribe to three different golf magazines. Each golf magazine competes with the others, but they can reach the exact same subscriber at the same time.

Direct competitors may be targeting your exact same market, but they can be allies to help all of you achieve greater success by cooperating.

While direct competitors are trying to reach the same market, an indirect competitor is somebody who is selling something different but targeting the same market. If you're targeting folks with back pain, an indirect competitor might be yoga lovers. They may be selling something different to your same customers, so they're still drawing away the attention from your market.

Indirect competitors are not bad. As a matter of fact, your indirect competitors may end up being your best business opportunities. The owners of your indirect competition should see you as synergistic, not threatening. Even though you're both targeting the same market, you're doing it with different products or services. As a result, people who like one product or service will likely want a related product or service as well.

If someone suffers from back pain, they may be interested in mattresses to relieve back pain, medicine that relieves back pain, stretching exercise instructions in books or DVDs that show how to relieve back pain, or devices you can wear to relieve back pain.

In many cases, one person will buy two or more similar products that all relate to providing relief from back pain.

The more indirect competitors in your market, the more likely you're in a market with lots of opportunities and interest.

Every market will have direct and indirect competitors, but all competition is good. The more competitors, the more it actually expands your universe by increasing the number of people looking for what you have to offer.

So don't freak out and think, "Oh my gosh! There are other people doing this!" If nobody else is doing something, that's a clue that there might not be any money in that market so you should probably pick a different market.

A great way to take advantage of both direct and indirect competitors is to invite them as expert panelists. If somebody sells something totally different than what you would ever think about selling, they can make a great advertiser. So someone could be a panelist, an advertiser, or both.

You want to be in the information products business. You don't necessarily need to sell physical products but information like e-books, coaching, and membership sites. So you might get advertisers who sell physical products. If their ad does well and they keep coming back to buy more ads, then you can look to get into the physical product business, too.

Quick Start Summary

Your action step for this chapter is to search Google using the primary keywords that define your market. Once Google returns some results, study the organic and paid listings.

Organic listings are the free listings, while the paid listings are the people who buy advertising from Google. Write down your top five direct and indirect competitors. Get on their lists (if you haven't already done that) so you can keep track of what they're doing.

Create a separate e-mail account (such as through Gmail) so that when you subscribe to your competitors, their messages go to a separate account that acts as a filing system. Now track everything you get from them because you can see who is making money in this business and exactly how they're doing it. This is more free competitive analysis.

With this list of your top five direct and indirect competitors, you'll know who might be your panelists, whom you might contact to do content swaps and syndications, and who might be potential advertisers. If someone's already advertising in Google, why wouldn't they advertise on your site as well?

At this point, you should have selected your market, determined its approximate size, created your customer avatar, and done your competitive analysis. Now you're ready to focus on creating your inbox magazine.

PART II

ANATOMY OF YOUR BUSINESS

And here is the prime condition of success, the great secret. Concentrate your energy, thoughts and capital exclusively upon the business in which you are engaged in. Having begun in one line, resolve to fight it out on that line; to lead in it. Adopt every improvement, have the best machinery and know the most about it.
—*Andrew Carnegie*

6

A Proven Business Model: If It Ain't Broken . . .

A French woman, upon seeing Picasso in a Parisian restaurant, approached the great master and insisted that he put down his coffee and make a quick sketch of her. When he was done, she took the drawing, put it in her handbag, and pulled out her billfold.

"How much do I owe you?" she asked.

"Five thousand dollars," Picasso replies.

"Five thousand dollars? But it only took you three minutes!" she exclaimed.

"No," Picasso answered. "It took me all my life."

I share this story with you because the trade secrets you're learning right now took me my entire career to learn over the past few decades. While there might be other ways to learn what I'm explaining in this book, I'm teaching you the best way I know how.

By now, you already have an idea what you want to cover. Now you have to figure out how to turn your marketable idea into a proven content model. The three best content models are as follows:

- Expert panel
- Single guru
- Faceless model

An expert panel typically consists of multiple content providers who are experts in their niche. The single guru content model

Figure 6.1   The Money and Markets site follows an expert panel model.

relies on one expert in a specific niche. The faceless model generally relies on an association or directory that uses the inbox magazine as a vehicle for displaying its own advertising.

WorkingMomsOnly.com clearly follows the expert panel model. Besides myself, I've got several people, including Mariel Hemingway, Marie Forleo, Brian Tracy, and Dr. Sears, just to mention a few. Another good example of the expert panel model is the Money and Markets site (see Figure 6.1). It's not just Martin Weiss but his whole panel, including Mike Larson and Bill Hall.

There isn't a general rule of thumb about how many people could be on your expert panel. With the Money and Markets site, there's one expert for every day. With Working Moms Only, there are many different topics that we cover, and I wanted specific people who were experts on those topics.

In the guru model, the inbox magazine is all about a single guru. A great example of that business model is the Ali Brown site.

Figure 6.2   A single guru business model site.

Ali is also a member of my expert panel for Working Moms Only, but her inbox magazine is primarily about her (see Figure 6.2).

The faceless model is much less personality driven and more marketing driven. Your local city newspaper site is an example of a faceless model (see Figure 6.3). Although the people writing columns may have their names and faces prominently displayed, the overall site is less about the people and more about the information.

The Pros and Cons of Each Business Model

So how do you choose which business model might be best for you? Let's go over the pros and cons of each (see summary in Figure 6.4). Then you can see which business model focuses on your strengths and the target market for your inbox magazine.

The biggest advantage of the expert panel model is that your experts give you free content in exchange for exposure and

Figure 6.3   A faceless business model site.

marketing to your community. You don't need to create or sell any of your own products to market since you're taking a cut of all the profits from sales your experts generate. In addition, with so many experts providing content, you don't have to spend much time creating new content yourself.

The expert panel model also elevates your brand and establishes your credibility in the eyes of the public. Notice on the WorkingMomsOnly.com expert page, I am positioned right on top. Directly underneath me is Academy Award winning actress Mariel Hemingway (see Figure 6.5). This quickly enhances my creditability with folks who may not be familiar with me yet.

Best of all, if one of your expert panelists sends out a promotion to his or her own community, you can ask, "How well did it do?" When you get the answer, you can extrapolate those results based on

Panel/Expert Pros and Cons

Pros

- Free content
- No product creation necessary
- No marketing resources necessary
- Elevating your brand
- Small time investment
- Have metrics and results ahead of time

Cons

- Scheduling
- Conflicting opinions
- Not always the expert's priority

Figure 6.4   Pros and cons of the expert panel model.

Meet the Experts

MaryEllen Tribby

MaryEllen Tribby is the proud Founder and CEO of WorkingMomsOnly, the world's leading newsletter and website for the empowerment of the working mom. Prior to founding WMO, MaryEllen was Publisher & CEO of Early to Rise where she was responsible for growing the business from $8 million in sales to $26 million in just 15 months. Before that, she served as President of Weiss Research where she led the company to $67 million in sales from $11 million in just 12 months.

Because of her impressive track record of generating revenues and profits, MaryEllen is known in the Information Publishing world as "The Money Honey." She credits a good part of her success to her traditional New York City publishing career. In New York, she ran divisions at Forbes, Times Mirror Magazines, and Crain's New York Business and had some of the best direct response marketing and business mentors in the world. Due to her superlative direct response and business building skills and her ability to "channelize" marketing campaigns, MaryEllen is a highly sought-after business consultant, speaker, and author.

Her first book which she co-authored with Michael Masterson is: *Changing the Channel: 12 Easy Ways to Make Millions For Your Business*. It hit #1 on Amazon.com within just 10 hours of its release.

MaryEllen currently resides in Boca Raton, FL with Patrick, her husband of 13 years, and their three beautiful children, Mikaela, Connor, and Delanie. You can usually find them soaking up the sun on the beach or at one of the kids' sporting events.

She is a firm believer in paying it forward; and hopes that all working moms will take advantage of this global community.

Mariel Hemingway

Mariel Hemingway is an actress, model, author, mother, and a leading voice for holistic and balanced living. As the author of three books: Finding My Balance, Mariel Hemingway's Healthy Living From the Inside Out, and her recently released, Mariel's Kitchen, she has established herself as one of the most knowledgeable and articulate voices in the Body, Mind, Spirit movement. She speaks comprehensively about greening yourself through living a healthy life style, eating well, slowing down, and creating sacred space.

Mariel is the granddaughter of author, Ernest Hemingway. She's best known for her roles in "Lipstick" and Woody Allen's "Manhattan." She has made 30 films, numerous television series appearances and has hosted several environmental and humanitarian documentaries.

Figure 6.5   The expert panel on Working Moms Only.

what you already know about your own community and determine if you would like to send that promotion to your community.

Now there are some drawbacks of an expert panel model. First, there's scheduling. You must make sure you get content from your panelists in a timely manner. This is why it is so important for you to "bank" your content (which we will cover soon).

However, a more challenging problem is dealing with conflicting opinions. For example, I have Dr. Al Sears on my panel, whom I admire a great deal and believe in his philosophy on alternative health. One time I had another health expert on my panel, but he was actually giving the exact opposite advice as Dr. Sears. Finally, I had to tell him, "I appreciate you so much, but I can't have you on my panel because I'm a believer in what Dr. Sears shares with my community, and I don't want to confuse my audience by giving them conflicting opinions."

This is an important matter because you're advocating for your community and saying, "This is what I believe in. This is what I'm going to put forward."

Of course, sometimes you may want panelists to disagree, such as an inbox magazine focused on the entrepreneurial market. Then you can tell your audience, "I realize that these two people disagree, but I want you to have both sides of the story. Test it out and see what works best for you." Even though people have conflicting opinions, you may still want to keep both of them and see whom your community resonates with the most. Very often in markets like this, there is room for both.

I've done that with exercise regimens because it's what works best for busy working moms. If she has only 12 minutes a day to do an exercise, then she may want to hear from Dr. Sears. If she can spend more time at the gym and enjoys it, then she may want to hear what other panelists have to offer about exercising.

The important point is that this is your business and you get to decide who plays in it. If there are conflicting opinions that create tension and confusion among your people, you've got to protect and advocate for them. It's no fun having to kick somebody off your panel, but your panel will constantly evolve so it's never a stagnant process.

If you are going to use the expert panel model, you might think, "I can't attract the level of experts that I want. Maybe I'll just do the guru model now and I'll do the panel later."

Keep in mind that you can still follow the expert panel model even if you don't have everybody that you want up front. People will come and go. Think of how a television network runs. One season you'll have a popular show, and the next season, that same show might not be as popular so it gets canceled. That just happens. Remember that you'll always keep discovering new talent that you'll want to bring on board. So your expert panel will constantly evolve.

What's a Guru?

Let's talk about the pros and cons of the guru model (see Figure 6.6).

On the pro side, you get to build your platform, and there's never a conflict of interest because it's all you, only you, all the time. You really can build a raving fan base.

The cons are that following the guru business model requires more investment in time because you have to write or produce all your content. This can be a huge business liability.

For example, when I worked at Weiss Research, our first inbox magazine was called Martin on Mondays. It was all Martin Weiss, all the time, so literally it was called the MOM for short.

Now imagine if something had happened to Martin or he simply did not want to work anymore. Losing Martin would have

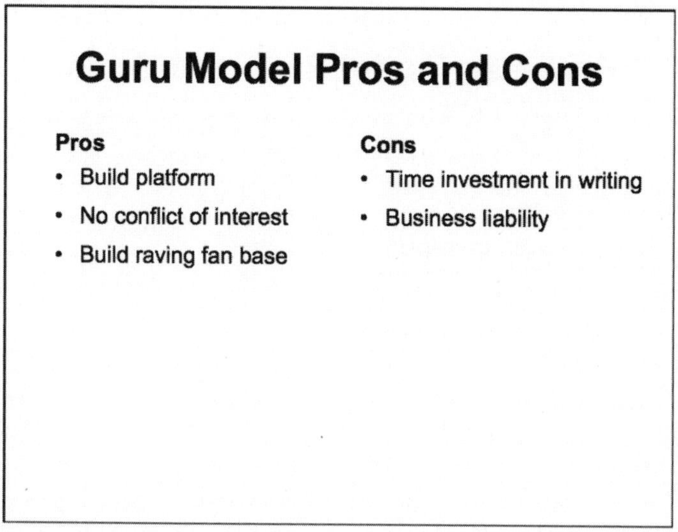

Guru Model Pros and Cons

Pros
- Build platform
- No conflict of interest
- Build raving fan base

Cons
- Time investment in writing
- Business liability

Figure 6.6   Pros and cons of the guru model.

meant losing the entire business. That's one reason we switched over to Money and Markets, with a whole expert panel that elevated everyone up to Martin's level.

If you're the guru type of person, you may want to focus on building up your persona and personality. You may not care because you want your business to be all about you, and that's fine as long as you understand the risk.

No Face—No Name

Now let's talk about the pros and cons of the faceless business model (see Figure 6.7). The advantage is that you can advertise anything you want and there's never any conflict of interest. The disadvantage is that there isn't any bonding mechanism. When you look at a faceless business model site, there isn't a face or personality on it, so it's harder for someone to get attached to that site. You can have more customer service issues just because of that.

For everyone starting an inbox magazine, the easiest business models are either the expert panel or the guru model. You aren't going to get much advertising right away because you're just starting out. Once you've established and have a list, you can start looking for a secondary source of income through advertising.

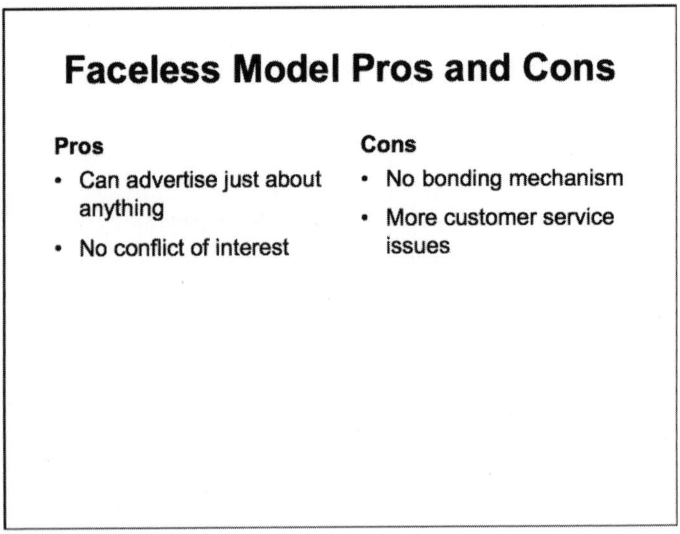

Faceless Model Pros and Cons

Pros
- Can advertise just about anything
- No conflict of interest

Cons
- No bonding mechanism
- More customer service issues

Figure 6.7   Pros and cons of the faceless model.

Remember, people really want to do business with people they know, trust, and like, and it's hard for people to know, trust, and like a faceless site. They want to hear from real people.

You can always transition from the guru model to an expert panel model and vice versa. That first inbox magazine called Martin on Mondays started off as a guru model, and then it became an expert panel model. There might come a day when Martin's not around anymore, so it could transition into a faceless model as its brand becomes better known. There could still be contributing expert panelists, but the brand will have the power at that point.

In the beginning, you really need a figurehead to build the brand power. The Oprah brand will probably go on past Oprah because she has built and continues to build experts under her like Dr. Phil, Suze Orman, and Dr. Oz. Now they all have multiple platforms of their own. But it really started as just her.

Show Me the Money

There are three proven ways to make money:

- The free model
- The paid model
- The hybrid model

The goal of the free model is to maximize your subscriber base and sell advertising within your inbox magazine (see Figure 6.8). First, you must determine your business model, and define a baseline so you know your dollars per issue. For example, if you have one ad per issue, will adding a second ad increase or decrease sales? When I headed up Early to Rise, we tested this over the years with the inbox magazine. We started with one ad, then two, three, four, and five. Finally, we determined that three was the optimal number of ads per issue.

You can sell your own product through a free inbox magazine, or just take a cut of the profits from sales of other people's products, which is known as affiliate revenue. If your inbox magazine has a large enough list, you can rent that list out to others. Use one method or multiple methods in combination to maximize the monetization of your inbox magazine.

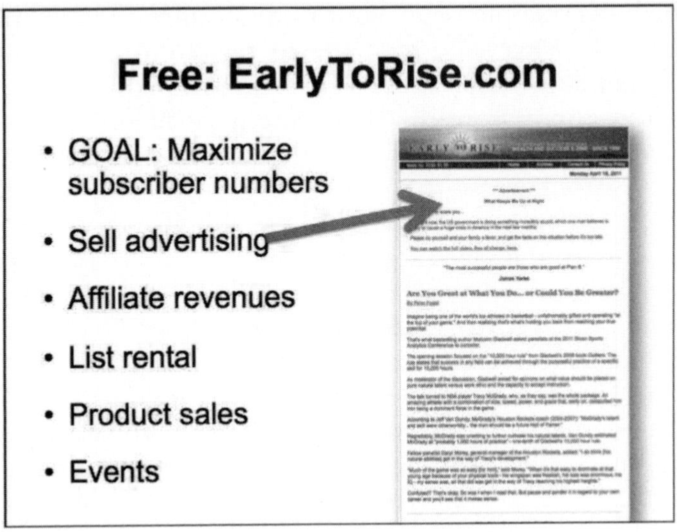

Figure 6.8   Making money from a free inbox magazine.

Basically, just ask yourself, "Do I want my inbox magazine to be totally free to my subscribers, where they don't pay anything? Then I'm going to make money selling advertising, getting affiliate revenue, renting out my list, or selling my own products, producing live events, or some combination of all of them.

With an expert panel model, you already have your advertising built in because your experts will be bringing their own products to sell.

If you want to offer a paid inbox magazine, that is more like a subscription business (see Figure 6.9). The problem can be getting started since people may be reluctant to subscribe to an inbox magazine that's brand new.

To overcome this problem, many people use a hybrid model that consists of a free inbox magazine that provides a lot of content, including links to videos. If people like the free content, then they're encouraged to subscribe to the premium content that costs money.

With this hybrid model, you might get people perfectly happy with the free content, so you can make money through advertising and other monetization methods. Then a percentage of people will pay for the premium content, so you get that additional income,

Figure 6.9   The paid model acts more like a subscription.

too. This premium content typically involves membership to access more information stored on your website.

For example, the Trade the Markets site targets day traders and anyone interested in trading stocks, currency, and commodities for a living. When you first visit the site, you can get free access to various articles explaining different strategies for trading during the day or over a longer period of time. All of these trading articles are free, so you can keep coming back and get a complete education on how to trade.

For many people, the free content may be all they want or need, but a percentage of those people will find the free content valuable and want something more. Maybe they want more detailed information about trading or trading in certain markets such as options or currencies.

That's when people will start looking at the premium content on the site. Since they're already happy with the free content, they'll often trust that the premium content will be worth the money. As a result, your free content helps bring in a steady stream

Figure 6.10   The hybrid model offers free and paid content.

of customers who eventually graduate up to your premium content (see Figure 6.10).

Now you have to decide if you want to go with the free model, the paid model, or the hybrid model.

If you are just starting out, the easiest, fastest, and cheapest way to start an inbox magazine is by following the panel model that is free. You can always change this later as you get experience and build up your subscriber list, but in the beginning, this takes the least amount of time to set up and captures the largest subscriber base from the start.

7

Naming Your Inbox Magazine: It's Got to Be Good!

The hard, cold truth is that names matter, and here's why. You may have heard of the expression "don't judge a book by its cover," but the reality is that people do judge books by their covers, and they do the same thing with inbox magazines, including yours. Here's why you want to carefully consider the name for your magazine.

Back in 1982, there was a book called *Astro-Logical Love* by Naura Hayden (see Figure 7.1). This book sold less than 5,000 copies and eventually went out of print. A man found this book while strolling through the remainder bin in a bookstore. He flipped through a few pages and thought that the content was fantastic but the name was terrible.

So he licensed the book from Naura Hayden and changed the title to *How to Satisfy a Woman Every Time . . . and Have Her Beg for More* (see Figure 7.2). When it was republished under this new title in 1998, it sold over 2.5 million copies, becoming a *New York Times* bestseller with the exact same content and the exact same author. All that changed was the title. That's why names matter.

A Name Can Make You or Break You

To come up with a name for your inbox magazine, brainstorm different ideas (see Figure 7.3). The more ideas you can generate, the more likely one of those ideas will be perfect. Even if you're

Published: 1982

Copies Sold:
< 5,000

Figure 7.1   *Astro-logical Love* sold poorly.

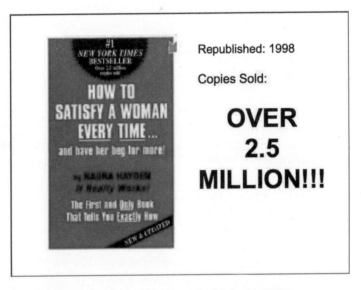

Republished: 1998

Copies Sold:

OVER 2.5 MILLION!!!

Figure 7.2   Just changing the name turned the same book into a bestseller.

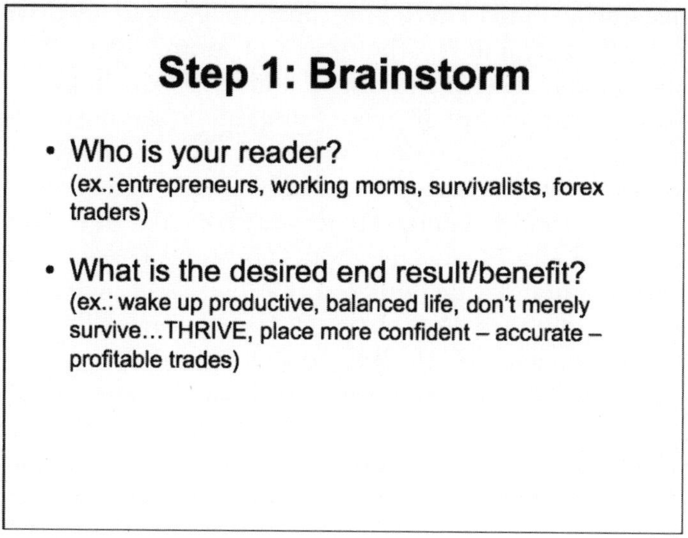

Step 1: Brainstorm

- ## Who is your reader?
  (ex.: entrepreneurs, working moms, survivalists, forex traders)

- ## What is the desired end result/benefit?
  (ex.: wake up productive, balanced life, don't merely survive...THRIVE, place more confident – accurate – profitable trades)

Figure 7.3   Brainstorming your inbox magazine name.

creating a free inbox magazine, treat it as if you're releasing a $5,000 training course. It deserves that much attention.

First, think about who your reader is. Are they entrepreneurs, working moms, survivalists, forex traders, or outdoor enthusiasts? You need to know without a doubt who that reader is.

Second, what is the desired end result of your inbox magazine? What's the benefit to your readers? With the Early to Rise inbox magazine, the goal was to help subscribers wake up productive, ready to get the most out of their day. With Working Moms Only, the goal is to offer readers tips and advice to achieve a healthier, wealthier, balanced, blended lifestyle. With an inbox magazine devoted to survivalists, readers don't just want to survive but thrive after any calamity.

Your inbox magazine name absolutely needs to describe your target audience and the most prominent benefit.

Consider Working Moms Only and its tagline: "Where passion, empowerment, and success meet." Does that say it all? The title describes the *who*, and the tagline describes the benefit.

Sometimes the name of the inbox magazine calls out to the market audience and the tagline calls out the benefit, but it can be the other way around. There's an inbox magazine called Deals for Mommy and its tagline is "The power of Mom." Here the tagline defines who the market is and the title describes the benefit.

Another example is an inbox magazine called The National Association of Entrepreneur Moms with the tagline "Empowering moms to consciously create a balanced life." This is actually a good example of a great inbox magazine that doesn't have a very good title or tagline.

Look at the names Working Moms Only and Deals for Mommy. Both contain punchy titles that jump at you right away. The third one's a real mouthful: The National Association of Entrepreneur Moms. Which one is easier to say and remember?

In your market, you may think that all the best names have been taken, so you may need to use synonyms and antonyms (see Figure 7.4). Visit sites like Thesaurus.com and Dictionary.com. Type in some of your name ideas and you can see the Latin and Greek derivatives.

Even if you come up with a clever name, you still need a tagline that calls out to your market because this further helps them to understand that you're targeting them.

Also think about rhymes and alliteration. Things like YouTube sounds fun. Double Your Dating is an example of memorable

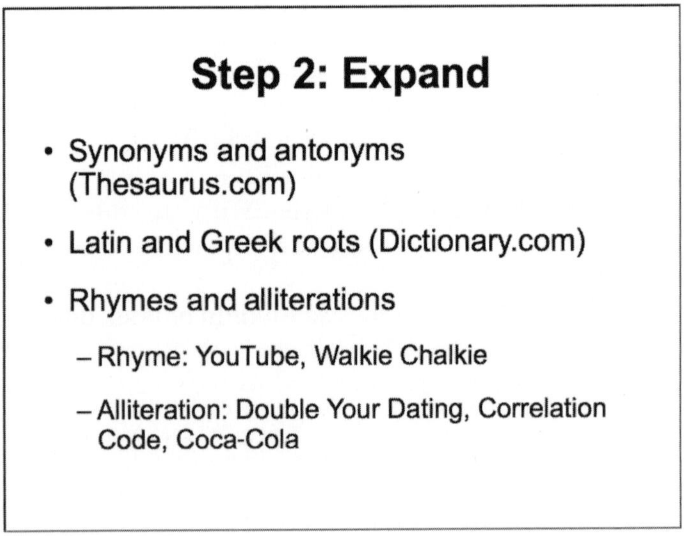

Step 2: Expand

- Synonyms and antonyms (Thesaurus.com)

- Latin and Greek roots (Dictionary.com)

- Rhymes and alliterations

  – Rhyme: YouTube, Walkie Chalkie

  – Alliteration: Double Your Dating, Correlation Code, Coca-Cola

Figure 7.4   Expanding variations of a name.

alliteration, much like Coca-Cola. If your title rhymes and includes some alliteration, such repetition can make your title memorable. Any time you have something memorable, it will stick in people's minds and will be more fascinating.

Of course, make sure that it works for your market. You don't want to be too cute in the financial world. Your title has to match your market.

Also make sure you eliminate any names that people can easily misspell and mispronounce (see Figure 7.5). Eliminate any names that are just too long as well as any name that sounds too generic. A financial inbox magazine called The Trading News is so overly generic that people probably won't remember what it is. That doesn't mean that your title can't be simple. Working Moms Only is simple but not generic. When you say Working Moms Only, that's saying this is only for working moms. The title calls out your group without being generic or too long. A good rule of thumb is three words or less, but definitely no more than four words.

Most important, make sure that your name isn't already taken. Before you fall in love with a name, do a Google search for U.S. trademarks by visiting the U.S. Patent and Trademark site (www .uspto.gov) and search for your title. If nobody else has it, you're

---

Step 3: Refine

Eliminate names that are:

- **Easily misspelled**

- **Generic** (ex. The Trading News)

- **Too long** (preferably three words or less, but no more than four)

- **Already taken** (Google: "US trademark search" and check GoDaddy.com for domain)

Figure 7.5   Refining a name.

probably fine (but check with an attorney to make sure), but if somebody has already registered that exact name, move on.

What you don't want to do is create a logo, invest in domain names and websites, start building a list, and suddenly find out that you've got to change the name of your entire business. That's expensive and confusing to your readers, which will hurt your e-mail deliverability rates as well as your credibility.

Once you've settled on a name, get it trademarked. It should cost only a few hundred dollars, and any attorney can file a trademark for you. Also, get a relevant domain name. If you can't get any relevant domain names, you may need to come up with a new title for the inbox magazine because you really want to brand the name of your inbox magazine since that's what people will search for. They're going to tell their friends, "Boy, I really love this Working Moms Only inbox magazine that I subscribe to." And they'll tell their friends they can get it at WorkingMomsOnly.com or just search for it on Google, Bing, or Yahoo!.

That's why you really need a relevant domain. Check GoDaddy .com and see if there's a relevant domain name available. It doesn't have to exactly match, but if you can't find a domain name that's very close, you might want to consider a new name.

Give the People What They Want

If you've ever heard of the *New York Times* bestseller *The 4-Hour Workweek*, here's a story about how the author, Tim Ferriss, came up with that name. Tim knew that his content was good, but he knew the vast majority of the book's success depended on the title.

Tim actually had half a dozen other names for his book, and "The 4-Hour Workweek" was not on the top of his list. But he knew that what he thought did not matter. The only thing that mattered was if the name resonated with the book buyers. So to test different book titles, he created a Google ad so that the title of the book was the ad headline and the subtitle was the body copy (see Figure 7.6).

You can do the same test with the name of your inbox magazine and also test different domain names to see which domain name gets the most clicks. Because of the limited number of characters you can display in a Google ad, this exercise will force you to come up with a short, concise name.

Figure 7.6   How Tim Ferriss tested the name of his book ahead of time.

Google's AdWords even has a split testing mechanism so you can test two different variations of your title to see which one gets the most clicks. The most popular one should probably be the title of your inbox magazine. This is ultra cheap and fast market research.

When Michael Masterson and I wrote our book *Changing the Channel: Twelve Easy Ways to Make Millions for Your Business,* he had a title that he really liked and I had a title that I really liked. Then one of our marketing assistants said, "What about just calling it 'Changing the Channel'?" At first we said no, but then we decided to test it using Google Ads. Michael Masterson's title lost, my title lost, and our marketing assistant's title won. Then we went on to sell thousands and thousands of copies of that book and hit number one on Amazon's best-selling list in the first 10 hours of release.

Is my ego bruised because my title didn't win? Absolutely not. It's never about your ego; it's about what resonates with your target audience. I'd rather be rich than right. The only marketing genius at the end of the day is the customer or the subscriber, so trust them.

Another way to test is to ask, "Does it pass the T-shirt test?" Peter Drucker said that your mission statement should be so concrete that it should be able to fit on the front of a T-shirt. That's exactly how I feel about the name of your inbox magazine. As you can see, Working Moms Only makes a great T-shirt title (see Figure 7.7). You can use your tagline with your title as well. In this case, I'd rather have the logo than my whole tagline on there.

Now think back to the name "The National Association of Entrepreneur Moms." Wouldn't that look a little bit ridiculous on a T-shirt? Even though they have a good newsletter with good content, the name isn't that great.

Give It a K.I.S.S.

If you have a whiteboard, or even a poster board, that you can put some place where you can easily see it, this is what I want you to do. Divide the whiteboard or poster board in half. On the left-hand

Figure 7.7   Testing if a name passes the T-shirt test.

side, write down some possible names. On the right-hand side, jot down some possible taglines.

Just focus on writing. Don't think about matching the taglines with your names right now. Just think about the "who" and the "benefit." The "who" is your target audience for your inbox magazine, and the "benefit" is what your tagline emphasizes.

Later, you can mix and match the names with the taglines. Just let the names and taglines come to you and write them down. When thinking about a name for your inbox magazine, stick to the K.I.S.S. strategy: keep it simple, sweetie.

The more names and taglines you write down, the more choices you'll have for finding the perfect name and matching tagline. You don't even have to finish this exercise in one sitting. Just jot down the ideas as they come to you, and by the end of the week you should have several great names and taglines that will be perfect for your inbox magazine and goals.

Design and Frequency: It's All about Engagement

Once you have a name for your inbox magazine and have defined your target audience, now you must determine the details of your inbox magazine (see Figure 8.1). How many days a week should you send out an issue? Which days should you send it? How long should it be? How do you decide what kind of sections you should have? Should it be text or HTML? Do you send the full inbox magazine or just part of it? Since these are the most frequently asked questions, let's jump right to it.

This may not be the answer you want to hear, but the answer to all six questions is really the same magic answer: your inbox magazine needs to fit your reader's needs and your schedule.

As a busy, working mom, my community of working moms couldn't read something every single day. That's just too much information, and they don't have the time.

For an inbox magazine about investing, each issue can come out daily. That's because the financial markets change every day, and if you skip a couple of days, you're doing a disservice to your customers, who need current information and advice. That's why the frequency of sending out your inbox magazine needs to be driven by your market.

If you're doing an inbox magazine about horoscopes and astrology, then sending it out daily would also make sense. Now, if you're doing an inbox magazine on scuba diving or skiing, you probably

Variables to Consider

1. How many days a week do I send out my inbox magazine?

2. Which days should I send it?

3. How long should it be?

4. How do I decide what kind of sections I should have?

5. Should it be text or HTML?

6. Do I send the full inbox magazine or do a partial push?

Figure 8.1   Questions to ask about your inbox magazine.

don't need to send out an issue every day. But because these folks are enthusiastic about scuba diving and skiing, you will want to deliver your inbox magazine at least once a week.

Sometimes you just have to add contrast to what everybody else is doing in the market. If everybody else in your market is blogging, you need to be different in good way. Maybe you need to be a little more formal or longer. It has to be driven by the market and the needs and wants of your ideal subscriber, but the general frequency should range from once a day to once a week. However, you always want to leave people wanting more instead of their not being able to read everything they already have.

Daily inbox magazines can be a disservice to your editors, your contributors, your experts, and to your advertisers. People might love it, but they just can't read it every day. If you make your subscribers feel overwhelmed and guilty for not reading everything, even if they're not paying for it, they'll eventually unsubscribe out of guilt.

Imagine if you joined a gym and every single day the owner of the gym called and said, "Hey, I noticed you weren't in today, what's going on?" And the next day it's, "Noticed you weren't in today, either. What's going on?" If they kept poking at you, you'd finally cancel, but if they just left you alone, you'd come when you could.

For Working Moms Only, I decided on a twice-a-week schedule because I knew that working moms needed this information more than just once a week. Now when I meet people, they tell me, "Yours is the only inbox magazine that I wait for, that I read every single time I get it." You're fighting for people's attention, and that's a scarce commodity these days.

When, Oh When

Now you may wonder, "What days should I send out my inbox magazine?" I send out Working Moms Only on Monday and Thursday because from working and testing for years on different inbox magazines, the highest open rates occur on Mondays. Also for Working Moms Only, Monday because is the start of the workweek after the weekend with the family. Then I chose Thursday because I specifically didn't want to do hump Wednesday. I wanted something closer to the weekend because there's often a quick tip about family and the weekend.

In general, Monday, Tuesday, Wednesday, and Thursday have much higher open rates than Friday, Saturday, and Sunday. Yet for certain markets like survival, I've tested and found that readership was highest on a Friday. For a foreign exchange (forex) inbox magazine, you may want to send it on Sunday, Monday, Tuesday, Wednesday, Thursday, and Friday since the forex markets are closed on Saturday and there's no trading going on. But the markets do open on Sunday, so your subscribers need this information on Sunday. Do you see how this is all driven by your market?

If you're doing a camping or a weekender type newsletter, then it makes sense to send it on the weekend. But, generally, if you're going to mail an inbox magazine once a week, send it out on a Monday, Tuesday, Wednesday, or Thursday.

Once you understand who your market is, it's easy to find out their reading habits, when they're at their computer, and when they open their e-mail messages. Don't forget that everyone can read an inbox magazine on a smartphone or tablet, so decide what works for you, and then test.

Once you settle on a day to send, you also need to consider the times to send. For a financial and investing inbox magazine, sending it at 5:00 A.M. makes perfect sense. Working Moms Only gets sent out by 5:00 A.M., as does Early to Rise. Your market will dictate when you need to send out your inbox magazine. To a lesser extent, your schedule can also determine the best time to send based on your lifestyle.

TheStreet.com is actually one of the only inbox magazines that I know about that goes out three times a day. They have Before the Bell, Midday Bell, and After the Bell editions because they follow the markets. Ultimately, you have to make a decision and then test to determine what your customers like best.

Plain Text or HTML—What?

For the actual format of your inbox magazine, the two main options are plain text or HTML, which is the programming language used to design web pages. For Working Moms Only, 1 like the graphical look of HTML, but for many other inbox magazines, such as Bob Bly's Direct Response Letter, the content appears as plain text.

When you're talking to women, they tend to care more about an inbox magazine that looks nicer. When you're talking to certain markets that are mostly men or more left brain, they really don't care what the inbox magazine looks like just as long as it contains solid information with important facts.

With plain text, you can only describe so much in words. With HTML, you can include nice photos and graphics to look more professional, more like a print publication.

Some people worry that their e-mails might get blocked if they send them out as HTML. That may have been true in 2003, 2004, and 2005, but today just the opposite is true. HTML e-mails, especially if they have images, actually get better e-mail deliverability than just straight text.

HTML is also far more versatile. You can include images that are clickable such as charts, top 10 lists, and infographics. The bottom line is that HTML, for the most part, will be more engaging. So to start, create your inbox magazine using HTML.

If you're concerned because you don't know how to build HTML e-mails, don't worry. There are so many outsourcing sites you can use for very little money. A site like Fivver.com will build a template for you for $5. So unless you've got a great reason to go with text, go with HTML.

Let's Push It!

Now, people often ask if they should send out the full e-mail or do a partial push. A full e-mail is when someone opens up their e-mail and sees your entire inbox magazine there in its entirety. A partial push is when they open up their e-mail and just see a paragraph there with a link that brings them to the entire issue.

Working Moms Only is full push so subscribers get the complete issue in their e-mail, but the Trade the Markets inbox magazine that you saw in the previous chapter is a partial push. When subscribers open their e-mail, they see a title and a paragraph or two, but it contains links to the website where the content actually appears.

People will do a partial push for several reasons. One of the biggest reasons is that it will drive subscribers to visit their website, which pushes up their Alexa ranking that measures how popular a website might be. For me, I wanted subscribers to get Working Moms Only in one click.

When we tested this at Early to Rise, our subscribers got very annoyed with the partial push. Even though they could read the same content on a website, they didn't want to make that extra click. For us, it wasn't about increasing the ranking of our website; it was about giving value to our subscribers.

You're also doing a disservice to your advertisers if you're forcing subscribers to click to receive the complete inbox magazine issue for the wrong reason. Another reason some inbox magazines do a partial push is that they want to train their subscribers to click. But what you really may be doing is giving them several places to click, therefore taking them off your page, distracting them with your site so the reader may never finish reading your content.

It's better to display the content so if somebody sees something they like in an ad or at the end of the article, that's when they click and leave the inbox magazine only to buy something.

In most cases, I recommend a full push unless you want to include video. Right now, you can't easily send a video that can play inside of an inbox magazine. You have to offer a link that takes people to a separate web page. That's why many financial trading inbox magazines use a partial push.

To increase e-mail deliverability, some people say, "If an e-mail is too long, then it's going to get blocked by spam filters and won't get through." Actually, longer messages get better deliverability than short messages because spammers send short messages. Spammers don't send out beautiful-looking newsletters. That's why Internet service providers (ISPs) give preferential treatment to e-mails that have more content in them. With Working Moms Only, we have a 99 percent deliverability doing a full push.

It Needs to Be Actionable and Useful

You may wonder, "How long does my inbox magazine need to be?" Basically, it needs to be as long as it needs to be.

If you're sending out a horoscope, it's going to be much shorter than if you're sending out advice and opinions. The average length of a Working Moms Only inbox magazine might range from 1,300 words to 2,200 words.

Your inbox magazine needs to be engaging without fluff. It needs to be actionable and useful at the same time, where nothing should be arbitrary. For Working Moms Only, I've defined the different sections and the approximate length (see Figure 8.2). They are exactly what is needed to get the reader engaged and fully satisfied. I always start with an introduction that's typically between 60 and 200 words. The purpose of the introduction is to get the reader excited about the issue.

Then I have a main essay that's typically between 1,000 and 1,400 words. Its purpose is to convey a single, useful, and actionable idea. Don't try to put too many ideas in a main essay. Just focus on one big idea.

My "Check It Out!" section is essentially my advertising section that ranges from 60 to 100 words. Its purpose is to get the reader to click on the link that brings them to the ad. The ad can be text or an image. For your own inbox magazine, you'll need to test what works best with your particular audience.

My "Quick Tip" section is designed for 100 to 200 words to give the reader a tidbit in 30 seconds because they're busy, working moms.

The "Look Who's Talking" section is meant to share what other people are saying about the Working Moms Only community, about me, and about the experts on our panel.

WMO Structure

Section	Length	Purpose
Introduction	60–200 words	To get the reader excited about the issue
Main Essay	1,000–1,400 words	To convey a single idea that is useful and actionable
Check It Out!	60–100 words	To get the reader to click on the link
Quick Tip	100–200 words	To give the reader advice that can be read within 60 seconds
Look Who's Talking	50–150 words	To share with the community
What Did You Think?	15–30 words	Solicited feedback

Figure 8.2   The basic structure of Working Moms Only.

The "What Did You Think?" section is to get feedback from my community.

This format works for me, but it's not the only format. The Early to Rise newsletter had three ads within it, a main essay between 1,000 and 1,400 words, and a little story section of about 600 words. So you have to decide what works for you.

Stick to Your Guns

Once you determine your guidelines, you need to stick to them. For example, my main essay must range between 1,000 and 1,400 words. If I get an essay from an expert panelist that's only 600 or 700 words, I won't run it.

People might ask, "Why does it have to be that long?" The reason is that when you're giving useful and actionable advice, it needs about 1,000 words to get the complete message across. Anything less will typically not do the job. Anything more than 1,400 words usually is not concise. Remember, you want your reader to keep coming back. You don't want readers to think that reading your inbox magazine takes too much time or doesn't give them the full picture.

Your Panache

Although I've given you guidelines for designing the format of your own inbox magazine, you must still test different designs for your own market and audience. But don't worry. Any decisions you make today, you can always go back and change in the future once you know what your audience likes.

Imagine if you had to go through these same steps with a printed magazine. You wouldn't be able to respond to feedback quickly, so you'd be stuck with a less-than-optimal design for a long time.

Just make a decision and get started with the basic guidelines provided. Then start testing and modifying what you have to see what might work better. It's a never-ending process of changing something, testing those changes, and trying to increase your results a little bit each time. You never have to make it perfect; you just have to get it done and in the hands of your subscribers.

9

Software and Systems: Technology Made Easy

Once you're ready to start sending out your inbox magazine, you need to focus on the details: software and systems. Don't worry, you won't need to know how to program a computer or even design a web page. All you need to know is what types of services you need to use and how they work. For me, this was one of the scary parts. But I soon found out that it didn't need to be. If I—a technological neophyte—can do it, anyone can do it.

The four services to look at include:

- AWeber.com
- 1ShoppingCart.com
- Infusionsoft.com
- iContact.com

These are the only four solutions I recommend, but you can shop for similar services, so don't feel that you have to use any of these. Just use these as a starting point.

AWeber is basically an e-mail auto-responder. People send you e-mail, and AWeber lets you decide how to automatically respond. For example, if someone signs up for your inbox magazine, you don't want to manually send out a reply because you might get 100 requests at a time or get a request for your inbox magazine in the middle of the night.

By using AWeber, you can automate everything. As soon as someone requests your inbox magazine, AWeber can store that person's e-mail address in your subscriber database and then send out a welcoming response. Each time you create an issue of your inbox magazine, use AWeber's HTML templates and instruct AWeber to send it out to your subscribers on the day and time you specify.

I started Workings Moms Only with AWeber.com because it's inexpensive, their e-mail deliverability is fantastic, and they offer beautiful, prebuilt HTML templates that are perfect for creating your inbox magazine. You'll literally be able to put your inbox magazine together and send it out within an hour. As you get better and more experienced, you can reduce this time to between 20 and 30 minutes.

AWeber is great for automating your subscriber list, but that's all it does. If you want to sell products, AWeber lacks any type of billing capability, so if you need to sell products or offer a paid premium option, you might want to use 1ShoppingCart.com or Infusionsoft.

1ShoppingCart doesn't have all the features of Infusionsoft, but it's easier to use and much less expensive. From my own experience, 1ShoppingCart's e-mail deliverability tends to be very good as well. I started with AWeber and 1ShoppingCart, and now I run Working Moms Only completely through Infusionsoft.

If you use 1ShoppingCart, you don't need AWeber because 1ShoppingCart also has an e-mail delivery feature that can collect leads, manage your subscriber list, and send off automated replies and inbox magazine issues. 1ShoppingCart may not be as advanced as AWeber with their automation tools, and they don't have a library of prebuilt HTML templates for creating your inbox magazine.

Infusionsoft works great for automating e-mail like AWeber but also combines the payment options of 1ShoppingCart, so it's an entire business management solution. However, Infusionsoft is more expensive and complicated to use. If you are just getting started, Infusionsoft may be more than you need.

I know someone who started an inbox magazine with 1ShoppingCart, and his business is up to $8 million dollars a year—and he's still using 1ShoppingCart. When I started Working Moms Only, I started with AWeber and 1ShoppingCart combined, so they work really well together.

The Bad You Need to Know

One huge drawback to AWeber is that it can't import data stored in other services. For example, if you start with 1ShoppingCart, Infusionsoft, or iContact, and later decide, "Hey, I want to try AWeber," you cannot directly import your captured names and addresses without forcing everyone to reconfirm their information all over again. When you do that, you're going to lose a good portion of your list.

If you start with AWeber, you can always pull your leads out and move them to 1ShoppingCart, Infusionsoft, or iContact, but if you start with 1ShoppingCart, Infusionsoft, or iContact, you'll never be able to move those subscribers into AWeber later on. AWeber is a great starting place but not a place to go back to.

Now iContact.com is similar to AWeber in that both offer automated e-mail responses. Like AWeber, iContact doesn't offer an online shopping cart or the advanced marketing features and business management solutions that Infusionsoft and 1ShoppingCart offer.

However, iContact can import names and e-mail addresses that you may have captured and stored in another service like Infusionsoft or 1ShoppingCart. Also, iContact offers a huge library of beautiful HTML templates you can use to create and design your inbox magazine. The drawback is that iContact is more expensive than AWeber. If you're just getting started, you may find iContact a bit more complicated than AWeber as well.

You Want to Stay Single

When you capture names and e-mail addresses to send out your inbox magazine, you need to be aware of spam complaints. To reduce the chance of spam, most services offer something called a single opt-in or a double opt-in.

A single opt-in is where you ask for someone's name and address once before you start sending e-mail. A double opt-in is where you ask for someone's name and address once, and then ask them a second time to verify this information before you start sending them e-mail.

Double opt-ins greatly reduce spam complaints because anyone who enters their name and e-mail address twice will be motivated to receive what you have to send them. Unfortunately, forcing people to enter their name and e-mail address twice also reduces the number of people willing to go through this double opt-in procedure, which simply puts more obstacles in the way of potential subscribers.

AWeber defaults to a double opt-in for creating your list of names and e-mail addresses, while other services like iContact default to a single opt-in. I recommend a single opt-in to make it easier for someone to give you their name and e-mail address. Then provide great content and always offer an unsubscribe button to reduce the problem of spam complaints.

In general, you can offer the exact same inbox magazine with the same type of offer, but a double opt-in will reduce the number of subscribers and make you less money every time.

When you set up with AWeber, the default will be a double opt-in. If you're willing to take the time, you can set up AWeber to switch from a double opt-in to a single opt-in.

For anyone just getting started with a free inbox magazine, the best and simplest solution is still AWeber. You can always move away from AWeber, but you can never move back, so you might as well start with AWeber. Then when you grow or start selling products, you can move to 1ShoppingCart or Infusionsoft.

Websites Have Never Been Easier

Now if you're going to create a website to promote your inbox magazine, the last thing you want is a static, old-fashioned web page. To change anything on such a static web page, you'll need to use a special web page designing program and then upload your pages to a server. It's not hard but it's clumsy, and not many people want to spend their time designing and editing web pages. The best website solution for avoiding this is WordPress.

First, if you go to WordPress.org, you can set up a website absolutely free of charge. Second, you don't have to know anything about designing a web page because you can use something called a WordPress theme that you can buy or get for free from the following sites:

- WooThemes (www.WooThemes.com)
- DIY Themes (www.DIYThemes.com)
- WordPress (http://wordpress.org/extend/themes)

Just search Google for "WordPress themes" and you'll find all you could ever want and more.

Basically, this is how you set up a WordPress site. You design the basic structure such as what you want to appear on your first page, what you want to appear on your second page, and so on. You can always add or delete pages at any time, so you can keep changing the structure of your website quickly and easily.

Each page can contain text and pictures. As you add or delete pages, WordPress automatically keeps track of your pages to create a menu. That way, people visiting your website can easily navigate to all the pages of your website.

Once you've designed your basic structure, you pick a theme. A theme simply displays your pages or content with a consistent graphical look. You don't need any graphical design skills to create a beautiful-looking website. All you need to focus on is creating the content, and the theme takes care of the visual look of your website automatically.

There are different types of themes you can use, but for promoting an inbox magazine, go with a WordPress magazine theme. A magazine theme makes your website resemble the layout of a magazine. By choosing different magazine themes, you can completely modify the appearance of your website in seconds without affecting your actual content one bit. That's what makes WordPress so powerful and easy to use.

Any time you want to modify your WordPress site, just log in from any computer. You can type or edit new content or upload new pictures. You could literally be on the beach with a laptop computer, and as long as you have an Internet connection, you could update your site from anywhere in the world.

No matter what type of theme you use, the most important feature is to place your subscription offer on the top or the upper right corner. Even though WordPress makes it easy for anyone, even those without any technical background whatsoever, to set up a website, you can always hire others to set one up for you. Then you can take advantage of WordPress to easily update and modify your site just by editing text or adding or removing pictures.

Opt Them In—Send It Out

Whether you want to set up a website yourself through WordPress .org or hire someone to do it for you, the point is to get started now. Your website will attract potential subscribers, and if they like what they see, they'll give you their name and e-mail address to receive your inbox magazine.

When they type their name and e-mail address into your WordPress site, those data get sent to AWeber, 1ShoppingCart, Infusionsoft, or iContact to store in a database. From that point on, everything is automated.

Subscribers receive their inbox magazine at a specific time and day, such as 5:00 A.M. every Monday and Thursday. All you have to do is focus on creating the content for your inbox magazine and let your website and services like AWeber take care of the details. It's really that easy!

CHAPTER 10

Don't Wait: Action You Can Take Right Now

Now that you've learned all the steps necessary to create your own inbox magazine, it's time to put it all together. There are five action steps you need to take right now:

Step 1: Determine your content model.

Step 2: Determine your monetization model.

Step 3: Create a title and tagline.

Step 4: Decide on a delivery schedule and format.

Step 5: Define the structure of your inbox magazine.

Action Step 1

For action step 1, determine your content model by writing down your pros and cons for each one (see Figure 10.1). When you're done, print out this out and circle instinctively which one you feel is best for you. The three choices are:

- Panel
- Guru
- Faceless

Remember, a panel model involves getting other experts to contribute content periodically. A guru model focuses solely on you. A faceless model emphasizes a company or organization.

ACTION STEP 1:

Determine your content models by writing
down your pros and cons.

(Circle one of the options below...)

Panel / Guru / Faceless

Figure 10.1   Determining your content model.

If you circle the faceless content model, ask yourself why. In
most cases, you should follow the panel or guru model unless you
have a really good reason for choosing the faceless model. Even if
you are worried about personal privacy, use a pen name. There's
nothing illegal, immoral, or unethical about that.

In general, I recommend the panel model. However, if you're
an author or celebrity or just want it to be all about you, go with the
guru model. The faceless model usually does not have the bonding
elements of the other two options. Subscribers do not feel emotionally connected. Therefore, the faceless model is usually best for an
existing organization, but it tends to make less money.

Action Step 2

For action step 2, determine your monetization model based on
the assets you have in place today (see Figure 10.2). The three
choices are:

- Free
- Paid
- Hybrid (free and paid)

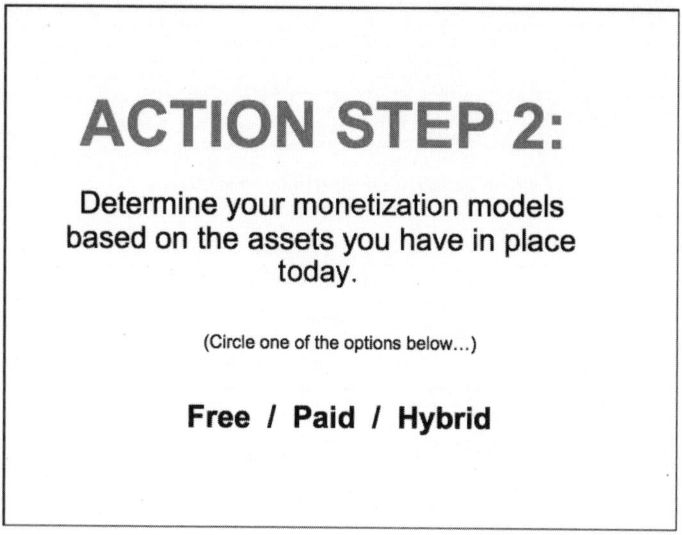

ACTION STEP 2:

Determine your monetization models
based on the assets you have in place
today.

(Circle one of the options below...)

Free / Paid / Hybrid

Figure 10.2   Determining your monetization model.

The paid model is really more of a subscription model like a magazine or a membership site. Unless you already have an existing site where people are willing to pay for your content, you probably shouldn't go with the paid option right now.

For the same reason, the hybrid model might not be a good option for you unless you're already offering premium content or a membership site. If you don't already have a stash of premium content you can sell, it's probably best to stick with the free model since it's easier to set up and get started. You can always switch to a hybrid or paid model later if you wish.

With the free model, you can find out what people actually want. If you don't have experience in the market, you're just guessing, especially if you start out with the paid model. Don't do that. It's hard to go back once you've launched a premium version, so start with the free model.

Action Step 3

For action step 3, come up with a working name and tagline (see Figure 10.3). A working name might not be your final name because you may want to test different names. Talk to your colleagues and do

ACTION STEP 3:

Come up with a working name and tagline.
(Fill in the blanks below...)

Name: _____

Tagline: _____

_____

_____

_____

Figure 10.3   Determining a name and tagline.

your research, but start with a working name. Write down what you feel right now, and then we'll take it from there.

Don't come up with just one name and tagline. Come up with as many as possible, and then double check to make sure there are no domain name or trademark issues with any of your working names. Also, test your name to see if it passes the T-shirt test. A name like Working Moms Only fits on a T-shirt. A name like Association of Female Entrepreneurs and Business Leaders will not.

Here's a little tip: leave a sheet of paper on your nightstand so that when you wake up at 2:00 in the morning with a great name (and you will), you can write it down and not try to remember it several hours later when you wake up.

Action Step 4

For action step 4, determine the delivery schedule and format of your inbox magazine (see Figure 10.4). Think about your frequency, the days you're going to send it, whether you want to write it in plain text or HTML, and whether you want to do a full or partial push. In most cases, you should send your inbox magazine out once or twice a week, any days between Monday and Thursday.

ACTION STEP 4:

Determine the delivery schedule and format for your inbox magazine.

(Fill in the blanks below...)

Frequency: _____

Days to send: _____

Text or HTML: _____

Full or partial push: _____

Figure 10.4   Deciding your delivery schedule and format.

Of course, that depends on your market. Definitely use HTML and full push unless you have specific reasons not to do so.

Action Step 5

In action step 5, determine the structure and deliverable content of your inbox magazine (see Figure 10.5). Basically, you want to define a format for your inbox magazine that offers consistent, predictable content. Working Moms Only has six sections, but your inbox magazine can have more or less. This is just a guide to help you get started.

Ask yourself the following questions:

- What is going to be my first section?
- How long is it going to be, and what's the purpose?

The purpose column makes sure that you actually think through each section so your inbox magazine provides consistent content. If the purpose of one or more sections is to make money, you don't want the purpose of every section to be making money. You need a balance between good content, good value, and asking

Structure and Deliverables

Section	Length	Purpose
1.		
2.		
3.		
4.		
5.		
6.		

Figure 10.5   Defining the structure of your inbox magazine.

people for money. Ultimately, the more you give, the more you're going to get.

You Are on Your Way!

Finish all these action items as quickly as possible while everything is still fresh in your mind. Make some decisions and don't linger. One of the most common traits of successful people is that they're decisive, so get going today!

PART

III

THE USEFUL AND THE ACTIONABLE

Business is not just doing deals; business is having great products, doing great engineering and providing tremendous service to customers. Finally, business is a cobweb of human relationship.
—*Henry Ross Perot*

CHAPTER

11

Building Your Panel: Content Is King

Your panel is what establishes trust among your subscribers. Remember, the panel model consists of multiple content providers, all experts in their particular field, with one primary expert or editor at the top.

If you're creating an inbox magazine, that primary expert or editor will be you. When you're in charge, you have to build the panel and make sure that every piece of content is worthy and useful to your community.

You want to list all your panel experts and their credentials to establish credibility for your inbox magazine and indirectly, for yourself somewhere on your website.

With Working Moms Only, I chose to list all the panel experts' credentials with their headshots on a separate page called "Experts." When you click on that navigation tab, it will take you here: www .workingmomsonly.com/meet-the-experts/ (see Figure 11.1).

Now readers can see who your experts are and what their specialty might be.

With the Money and Markets inbox magazine, Martin Weiss is truly the figurehead endorsing the rest of his panel. Notice that he has a full shot of himself, but every expert simply has a headshot and a much smaller biography (see Figure 11.2). Such a large picture might not work for other types of inbox magazines, but they can absolutely work for certain niches so you have to know your market.

Remember that as the publisher of your inbox magazine, you're the top expert. You're always on top, but your association with

MaryEllen Tribby presents

WorkingMomsOnly.com®

Where Passion, Empowerment, and Success Meet

🏠 Home

About   Experts   Look Who's Talking   Resources   Shop   Events   News

Meet the Experts

MaryEllen Tribby

MaryEllen Tribby is the proud Founder and CEO of WorkingMomsOnly, the world's leading newsletter and website for the empowerment of the working mom. Prior to founding WMO, MaryEllen was Publisher & CEO of Early to Rise where she was responsible for growing the business from $8 million in sales to $26 million in just 15 months. Before that, she served as President of Weiss Research where she led the company to $67 million in sales from $11 million in just 12 months.

Because of her impressive track record of generating revenues and profits, MaryEllen is known in the Information Publishing world as "The Money Honey." She credits a good part of her success to her traditional New York City publishing career. In New York, she ran divisions at Forbes, Times Mirror Magazines, and Crain's New York Business and had some of the best direct response marketing and business mentors in the world. Due to her superlative direct response and business building skills and her ability to "channelize" marketing campaigns, MaryEllen is a highly sought-after business consultant, speaker, and author.

Her first book which she co-authored with Michael Masterson is: *Changing the Channel: 12 Easy Ways to Make Millions For Your Business*. It hit #1 on Amazon.com within just 10 hours of its release.

MaryEllen currently resides in Boca Raton, FL with Patrick, her husband of 13 years, and their three beautiful children, Mikaela, Connor, and Delanie. You can usually find them soaking up the sun on the beach or at one of the kids' sporting events.

She is a firm believer in paying it forward; and hopes that all working moms will take advantage of this global community.

Mariel Hemingway

Mariel Hemingway is an actress, model, author, mother, and a leading voice for holistic and balanced living. As the author of three books: Finding My Balance, Mariel Hemingway's Healthy Living From the Inside Out, and her recently released, Mariel's Kitchen, she has established herself as one of the most knowledgeable and articulate voices in the Body, Mind, Spirit movement. She speaks comprehensively about greening yourself through living a healthy life style, eating well, slowing down, and creating sacred space.

Mariel is the granddaughter of author, Ernest Hemingway. She's best known for her roles in "Lipstick" and Woody Allen's "Manhattan. She has made 30 films, numerous television series appearances and has hosted several environmental and humanitarian documentaries.

Dr. Al Sears, MD

Dr. Al Sears, MD currently owns and operates a successful integrative medicine and anti-aging clinic in Florida with over 20,000 patients. His cutting edge therapies and reputation for solving some of the most difficult-to-diagnose cases attract patients around the world.

After entering private practice, Dr. Sears was one of the first to be board certified in anti-aging medicine. Today he is a diplomate of the American Board of Anti-Aging Medicine. As a pioneer in this new field of medicine, he is an avid researcher, published author and enthusiastic lecturer.

Dr. Sears is board certified as a clinical nutrition specialist and a member of the American College of Sports Medicine (ACSM), the American College for the Advancement in Medicine (ACAM), the American Medical Association (AMA), the Southern Medical Association (SMA), the American Academy of Anti-Aging Medicine (A4M) and the Herb Research Foundation, (HRF). Dr. Sears is also an ACE certified fitness trainer.

Since 2001, he's published over 500 articles and 6 books in the fields of alternative medicine, anti-aging and nutritional supplementation - with a readership of millions spread over 23 countries. You can visit him at: www.mypureradiance.com and www.alsearsmd.com.

Forbes Riley

Figure 11.1   Working Moms Only partial list of panel experts.

Figure 11.2   Money and Markets highlights the publisher over the rest of the panel.

others adds further credibility to both you and your inbox magazine. Subscribers will think that if you know a famous and powerful person, then the person running the inbox magazine must also be important and credible.

On the panel of Working Moms Only, you'll see that the first expert underneath me is Mariel Hemingway, an Academy Award–nominated actress who also had a huge modeling career. However, the real reason why she's on my panel is that she's an expert in healthy cooking and healthy foods. That's important for my audience of working moms, but of course, her celebrity status doesn't hurt.

Three Easy Steps for Putting Your Panel Together

There are three basic steps to putting together your panel (see Figure 11.3).

Step 1: Brainstorm a List of Potential Panelists

First, brainstorm a list of potential panelists. Don't limit yourself; contact the people you truly believe can add valuable insight and knowledge that your community will want to know about.

Start with your inner circle first. Believe it or not, you know more people than you think. Just write down everybody that you know and everybody you've worked with in business. I first met many of my panelists from doing business with them over the years, so it just made sense.

There's no limit to the number of people you can put on your panel, but don't go nuts and put 50 people on there because that will look ridiculous.

Also, don't worry if most people in your inner circle aren't major celebrities. As you get yourself established, you can eventually contact well-known people. When you're just getting started, you just need the best people you can get.

Some of the best people to target are authors and product creators. When I ran Early To Rise, I had Tim Ferriss on my panel before he became a huge celebrity. His book had just come out;

Building Your Panel

Step 1: Brainstorm a list of potential panelists.

Step 2: Contact each panelist with a request for content.

Step 3: Convert content providers into panelists.

Figure 11.3   The three steps to building your inbox magazine panel.

I loved it and contacted him. We met in New York over breakfast, and that's how he got on my panel. As his popularity and credibility grew, it made Early To Rise look even stronger.

So go after authors. They're not that difficult to get, they want to publicize their book, and they can create content just by pulling snippets of useful information out of their book chapters.

Besides authors, another type of person to target is product creators because these people already have something to sell. An important way to monetize your inbox magazine is by selling your panelist's products.

With authors, it's easy to make information products out of their content just by changing a few things. So you've got built-in product potential with authors as well.

If you don't know any authors or product creators personally, don't worry. It's surprisingly easy to find and contact them. Three websites to look for such experts are:

- RTIR.com
- eHow.com
- EzineArticles.com

RTIR.com　RTIR stands for Radio TV Interview Report, which is the site (www.rtir.com) where big TV and radio shows look for guests and celebrities to bring to their audiences. This is the site where the *Today Show, Good Morning America,* and even Howard Stern look for interesting guests (see Figure 11.4).

Basically, the way RTIR works is that experts pay to get listed on the RTIR site. Then anyone, such as the producers in charge of booking guests for the *Howard Stern Show* or *Good Morning America,* can find a guest that matches a topic they want to talk about.

Once you're on the RTIR site, you can click on a category or search for keywords to look for people with expertise in a certain field. Then read through the different listings to look for interesting topics currently being promoted by these experts.

To start using RTIR, click on the little fancy button to the right-hand side that asks, "Need to find a guest?"

There are a couple of ways that you can search. You can type a keyword into the search box, or you can search by clicking on a category such as education, environment, family, food, health and fitness, how to, or humor (see Figure 11.5). Chances are good that you're going to find something that relates to your topic.

Figure 11.4   Anyone can visit the RTIR site to look for experts in specific topics.

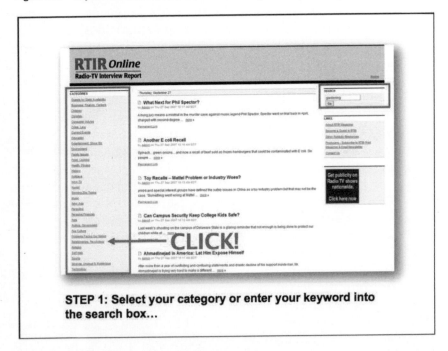

Figure 11.5   Narrow your search to specific categories.

If you click on a category, you'll have to narrow that broad category into a more specific topic. For example, if you want to find an expert in dating or singles, you might search for the relationships and psychology category. Then you might find specific topics such as, "As seen on FOX and CNN"; "Winner, Loser, or Psycho?"; and "How to Screen Your Online Date."

That topic would make an interesting article title. If you needed an article about online dating, this expert would have good information on how to screen people to make sure they are not serial killers or psychopaths.

Once you find a topic that seems interesting, click the More button (see Figure 11.6). In this example, this expert has already been featured on FOX and CNN, so you could promote their credibility with the media in your inbox magazine.

In this example, Stephanie Alexander is an online dating expert who has been answering questions about the way men use, abuse, and scam women on the Internet. She founded the site Womansavers.com, which is a database that compiles and profiles

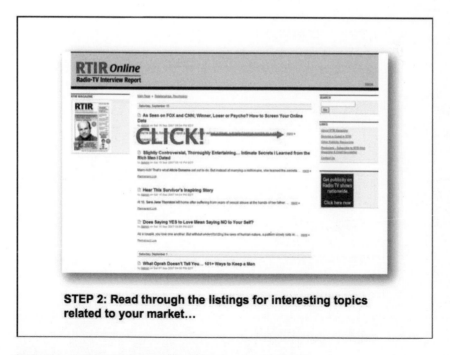

STEP 2: Read through the listings for interesting topics related to your market...

Figure 11.6   Look for interesting topics within your chosen category.

more than 20,000 abusive and cheating men, so she's obviously interested in promoting this website.

In addition, she's authored over 50 articles on relationships and dating, and has a report called "Sex, Lies, and the Internet." Her site's been featured in *Esquire* magazine, so she has tons of credibility. By visiting the RTIR site, you can even find her contact information such as a phone number or e-mail address (see Figure 11.7).

Just by following these simple steps on the RTIR site, you can quickly find somebody with good content who probably has a product to sell. If you offer them an opportunity to promote their products through your inbox magazine, that person might just say yes and you've just added a credible expert to your panel.

The best part about searching the RTIR site is that you don't have to become a member or even pay for anything. Just look for the experts you want and contact them directly.

I taught one of my students how to do an inbox magazine. She developed her own information product and then visited the RTIR site to look for panelists, and then she snagged a celebrity to be

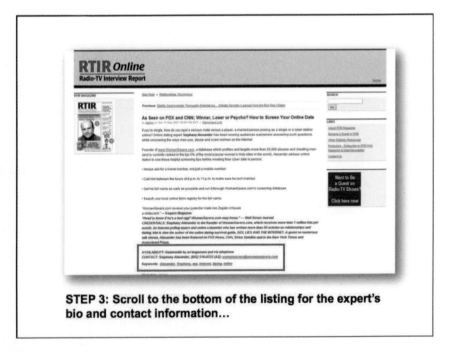

STEP 3: Scroll to the bottom of the listing for the expert's bio and contact information...

Figure 11.7   Contact the expert you like best.

part of her information product. You'll be surprised at how many impressive people you can find on RTIR that can give you immediate credibility.

If you look on WorkingMomsOnly.com, you can see the line where it says, "MaryEllen and her experts have been featured in:" followed by icons and logos from FOX, CNN, Lifetime, ABC, and the *Wall Street Journal.* All the exposure from your panelists lends credibility to your site. When you start gathering your own panelists, you can start putting logos like this on your site as well to piggyback off their previous success and credibility. Most important, you want people who have different credentials than you because it makes you and your site stronger.

By browsing through the RTIR site, you can find the highest-quality experts without having to hunt for their contact information. These people want to be contacted. You could probably find everybody you want for a panelist just using this site alone.

If you still haven't picked your market, just browse through the RTIR site to get ideas for what types of topics are out there, what people are writing about, and what people are looking for.

eHow.com   Another way to find experts for your panel is through eHow.com, which works much like RTIR. The main difference is that, unlike RTIR, people on eHow aren't paying to be listed. Most people on eHow are either posting free content or actually getting paid to write.

In most cases, these folks want to be contacted and would most likely love to have their content appear in other places, but it's not like RTIR. eHow doesn't necessarily want you contacting their experts because they'd rather force people to visit eHow to read this content.

When you visit eHow, you can see that they offer six main categories: family, food, health, home, money, and style. You'll need to click on their links to browse the articles and videos in each category (see Figure 11.8).

For example, let's say you wanted to target the health and fitness market. Go to eHow, click the health category, and search for fitness and nutrition. Not only can you find people who have written articles about fitness and nutrition, but you can also find people who have created videos as well. Now you get to see what these people look like and what they sound like.

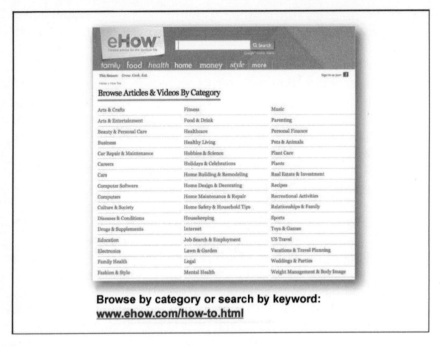

Figure 11.8   eHow lets you search by category or keyword.

Once you find one or more experts in a particular category, you may notice that eHow lists their name but does not provide any contact information like RTIR. For example, one expert on eHow is a woman named Leslie Mueller (see Figure 11.9). If you watch her video and like what you see, how can you get in touch to invite her to contribute to your inbox magazine or be part of your panel?

To find someone, just use Google and type in that person's name and expertise such as "Leslie Mueller fitness." By typing in an expertise, you avoid Google's finding all the Leslie Muellers in the world.

Just a quick search on Google will find someone's other sites such as their LinkedIn profile or Facebook page (see Figure 11.10). For example, Leslie Mueller also runs Indoorcycleinstructor.com, which may be a membership site, which indicates she could have something to sell.

Finding an expert's social media listing can be especially important because many experts don't check their own e-mail, but they do check their own Facebook messages or LinkedIn messages.

STEP 1: Locate an expert with a large number of quality videos/articles related to your topic…

Figure 11.9   eHow helps you find people, but not how to contact them.

STEP 2: Enter the expert's name into Google to find a home page or social media listing. (HINT: Facebook messages get the best response rates…)

Figure 11.10   Search for an expert using Google.

If you can't find someone through Google, search for them in Facebook or LinkedIn.

Here's an interesting insight on how eHow works. A company called Demand Studios (www.demandstudios.com) owns eHow and displays information for writers or video producers to produce content for eHow and make money.

Most writers earn between $15 and $20 an hour to write an article. If someone wants to write their own articles, they'll be paid on a revenue share basis, which is how the majority of writers make money on eHow.

Keep in mind that eHow doesn't allow anyone to repost content that they've written and posted somewhere else. All content on eHow must be 100 percent original exclusively for eHow. Even though eHow gets numerous visitors every day, most writers just make a fraction of advertising revenue generated by the eHow site. As a result, most people aren't creating content for eHow to get rich. They're creating content for eHow mostly to publicize themselves or their businesses. These are the types of people who would be open to a publishing deal working with you and your inbox magazine.

Remember that the structure of your inbox magazine might contain a main essay between 1,000 and 1,400 words. Guess how long that takes for an experienced writer? Under an hour, which means if you need help creating content, you can pay someone about $15.

Obviously, making $15 an article isn't going to get too many people excited, but what will get them excited is if you offer them access to your list on a regular basis. If they contribute articles independently or as a panelist, they'll gain credibility with your subscribers and be able to sell their own products to them. When experts see this possibility, it looks far more appealing than just getting a $15 check for one article.

EzineArticles.com   For a third source to find experts, visit EzineArticles .com. Ezine Articles can be fantastic for finding articles (see Figure 11.11). However, don't do what most people do and visit Ezine Articles to copy an article and plop it in their inbox magazine. You really need to make sure that you are getting good, hard-hitting content. If you just go to Ezine Articles and slap in any article that seems close to your topic, you will lose subscribers in a hurry.

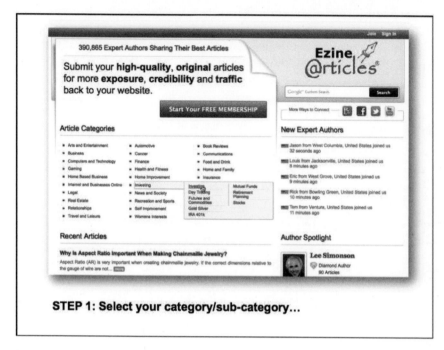

Figure 11.11   Ezine Articles can be a great place to find experts.

The best way to use Ezine Articles is to find experts. Visit Ezine Articles and select a category such as investing (see Figure 11.12). Within this category, select a more specific topic such as gold and silver. That pulls up a page that looks something like this. At first glance, you may see hundreds of articles. So how do you find the best authors who actually write a lot as real experts?

Ezine Articles doesn't make finding the best authors obvious, but it does offer a link that lists top authors for every category. Click on that link and you'll see a list of authors along with the number of articles they've contributed (see Figure 11.13).

Don't just look for the person who has written the most articles. Look for their status, which can range from Basic Plus to Platinum or Diamond. What you need to understand about these different statuses is that you can buy your way into Basic Plus or Platinum, but you can't buy your way into Diamond status. The only way to get Diamond status is to earn it by writing good, solid, quality articles that other people have reviewed.

Figure 11.12   Finding the top authors in a category.

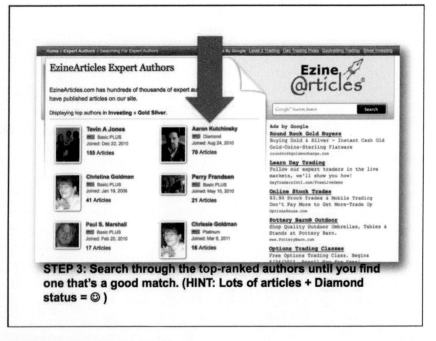

Figure 11.13   Viewing the most prolific authors.

What you want are experts who write lots of articles and have Diamond status. That doesn't mean that you can't contact somebody who doesn't have Diamond status. Do a little research, and if they offer good information, contact them (see Figure 11.14).

Most important, look at each author's picture to make sure it's appropriate to your market. A picture of an author with his wife and kid might be fitting for a family market, but that same picture wouldn't look as appropriate for the financial market.

When you find an author you like, click on his picture to find more information about him. Ideally, you want someone who has something to sell and definitely has an opinion. You don't want people writing boring, tepid content. You want people who have something to say and aren't afraid to express it.

They don't have to agree with you necessarily, but they do need a strong opinion. Also examine their articles. If someone writes only about finances or investment topics, he's probably serious about his information. If someone's writing articles about everything from financial advice to video games, that person probably isn't a true expert.

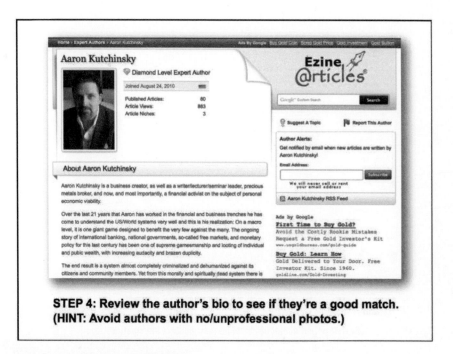

Figure 11.14   Research potential authors.

If you like a person, look for his website and blog links. You can contact him through his own website or by commenting on his blog (see Figure 11.15). Just write something like, "Hey, this isn't meant to be a blog comment, I'm just trying to get hold of Aaron. I have something I want to talk with you about if you can check your e-mail." That will probably get read. You can also contact people through their LinkedIn or Facebook pages.

Don't forget about authors, since authors love to talk about their books. Make sure you've read one of their books before contacting them. That way you can tell them, "A, B, and C will really resonate with my audience."

Also look for regular contributors to industry journals or magazines. If you're targeting a niche that you're passionate about, you probably already know who the experts are in that field.

In any field, there are likely Internet forums where people swap messages and ideas. Look for the people who are moderating these forums and being controversial because you want people who have something to say.

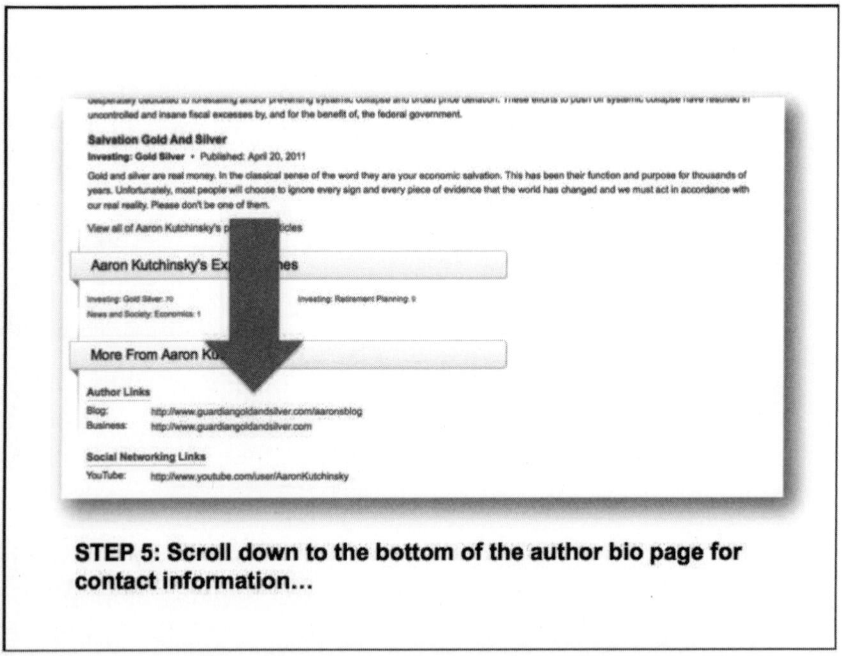

STEP 5: Scroll down to the bottom of the author bio page for contact information…

Figure 11.15   Research potential authors and find their contact information.

Just be careful about contacting somebody who's overly divisive. Some people are just mean and nasty, and if they're that abusive to others in a forum, they'll probably be just as mean and nasty to you. There's a big difference between being opinionated and having something to say, and being troublesome and nasty. It all comes down to professionalism and respect. You can have heated discussions with other people in the industry and disagree vehemently, but at the end of the day, you can still shake hands and be friends.

Radio and TV show hosts can be another great source for experts. If you are really passionate about something, you should go to industry conferences and listen to different speakers to make contacts. I first met Mariel Hemingway at a conference, and we became friends. When you promote your inbox magazine as a cause to serve a specific audience, most people want to be helpful.

Here's the big rule of thumb, though, especially when you're targeting celebrities. Wait until your inbox magazine is established with at least about 5,000 subscribers before you contact someone really well known. To make someone's effort worthwhile, you need at least 5,000 people.

If you're just getting started, you might want to hold off contacting major celebrities. You should have other panelists that celebrities will recognize. If you contact them too soon, they may think you're not professional enough.

The big difference is that experts you find on RTIR, eHow, and Ezine Articles want to be contacted. However, celebrities aren't necessarily putting themselves out there in hopes that people will contact them or help distribute their content.

Step 2: Contacting Potential Contributors—The Right Way

When you contact potential panelists or contributors, let them know the type of article you'd like from them, how many words it should be, and, most important, what's in it for them (see Figure 11.16).

When you make contact, each request should be personalized to that person. Never send a mass e-mail because that shows a lack of respect. Your first request should also be for content only, not to become a panelist. Remember, you are just meeting somebody for the first time.

Step 2: Making Contact

- Each request should be personalized to the potential panelist (NO MASS E-MAILS!!!).

- First request is for content, not to become a panelist.

- Compliment the individual but don't kiss their butt (positioning is still important).

- NEVER include a request for an ORIGINAL article in the first contact.

- Keep it short and simple.

Figure 11.16   How to contact potential contributors.

A good analogy would be a guy walking up to someone in a bar and immediately asking them, "Will you marry me?" Instead, you'd want to get to know each other. That's what you're doing when you ask for content.

Be sure to compliment the individual, but don't overdo it since that will make you come across as fake and phony. Your compliments should always be authentic and sincere. You should know what to say before you contact anyone. Your communication should come from a position of respect, not from the position of a fanatic.

I've had people approach me after I've spoken and say something like, "Oh, I love you so much, you are so great, you are so awesome, I can't believe I am talking to you right now." I know that people are just trying to be nice and complimentary, but when you approach someone from the standpoint of "I can't believe I'm talking to you," you place yourself so far below them that it would be awkward to ask them to partner with you. Be respectful and professional.

I once had a meeting with George Ross, who is Donald Trump's right-hand man and even appeared on Donald Trump's TV show, *The Apprentice.* I didn't shake his hand and say, "Oh my gosh. I loved you on *The Apprentice.* You were so funny when you fired people."

Instead, I just said, "I would love to hear about your years at NYU. I went to NYU, too." I just wanted him to make sure I knew about him, that I did my research and give us a certain connection. Now we could talk about it, and then get down to business.

Most important, never request an original article in your first contact. Please notice the word *original.* You just want to request an article and get right to the point.

Now here's an example of how not to make contact (see Figure 11.17). You don't want to contact somebody and say, "Hi, I'm looking for top experts in your field to be on a panel for my inbox magazine. The greatest inbox magazine ever." Number one, we aren't going to be asking them to be on a panel.

You also don't want to boast, "My inbox magazine is one of the best in the industry. You'll get a ton of free exposure. Plus, I'm going to have an affiliate program at some point, and if you promote my products, you get to keep 50 percent of every sale. The editorial guidelines for each article is below, and I'll need a commitment of at least one original article from you a month. Please respond to me within 48 hours or I'll be forced to open your spot to another possible competitive expert in your field."

What's wrong with this?

How **NOT** to Make Contact

I'm looking for top experts in your field to be on a panel for my inbox magazine, _____.

My inbox magazine is one of the best in the industry so you'll get a ton of FREE exposure. Plus, I'm going to have an affiliate program at some point, and if you promote my products you'll get to keep 50 percent of every sale!

The editorial guidelines for each article is below, and I'll need a commitment of at least one original article from you a month. Please respond to me within 48 hours or I'll be forced to open your spot to another (possibly competitive) expert in your field.

Sincerely,
Silly Nilly

Figure 11.17   How not to contact an expert.

First, it's all about the sender. There's nothing appealing for the expert. When asked the right way, most people will be happy to help. Nobody wants to say, "I helped you, now you better reciprocate and help me." When you say, "My inbox magazine is one of the best in the industry, so you will get a ton of free exposure," they won't care. Plus, you are just starting out and want to be honest. When you tell people that, it makes you sound like a total amateur.

Also, don't mention an affiliate program if you don't have one yet. Nobody cares about the percentage if you don't have an affiliate program up and running.

Don't attach any editorial guidelines at the first contact because you don't even know if that person will say yes to you or not. Don't try to get any commitments in the first contact.

Definitely don't say something like, "Please respond to me within 48 hours or I'll be forced to open your spot to another possibly competitive expert in your field." That comes across as arrogant, threatening, and unprofessional.

Here's a better way to do this (also see Figure 11.18):

"Hi, _____ [state that person's name]. My name is _____, and I publish an inbox magazine targeted at _____ [tell them the market it's targeted at].

Initial Contact Script

Hi _____,

 My name is _____ and I publish _____, an inbox magazine targeted at [your market]. Every now and then I like to profile a new industry expert for my subscribers, and after reading your book/product/article/etc., _____, it's clear that you'd be an ideal fit for my readers.

I wouldn't need any original content from you or anything like that. In fact, after reading some of the articles you've already written I'd be honored if you'd simply allow me to republish one of those.

Please let me know if you're able to help me out. My next issue is scheduled to go out on [next issue date], and I'd love to have you in that one.

Thanks, and I look forward to your reply,
[YOUR NAME]

Figure 11.18   A sample script to contact experts.

Every now and then I like to profile a new industry expert for my subscribers, and after reading your book/product/article, it's clear that you'd be an ideal fit for my readers."

First, you've acknowledged that you've read his books or articles and you've called him by name. Once you've gotten someone's attention, you can explain why you're contacting him:

"I wouldn't need any original content from you. In fact, after reading some of the articles you've already written (and now would be a good place to drop in some of those article titles), I'd be honored if you'd simply allow me to republish one of those."

Again you're not asking for original content right now, and you're definitely not sending him any type of editorial guidelines. What you are saying is that you'd like permission to copy and paste an existing article to publish in your inbox magazine, so there's literally no work you need from that expert. He is simply leveraging his existing content and getting it out to a broader audience. After explaining why you're writing, conclude with a request for action:

"Please let me know if you are able to help me out. (Those words right there are crucial because people enjoy helping other people.) My next issue is scheduled to go out on _____."

You might mention that your next issue is scheduled on a certain date and then give him at least a week to respond, even though all you're doing is copying and pasting his information.

With this approach, you first acknowledged his work in a respectful tone, you don't ask him to do any extra work, and you ask for his help with a very soft deadline.

That's the entire e-mail—three or four paragraphs followed by a hard-to-refuse offer without boasting about your own greatness. If someone's even remotely interested, he'll click on the link to your site and check it out. If it looks professional, he will likely say yes to some free exposure. Don't tell him that he'll get free exposure. He knows that. Telling him only cheapens your message.

After your name, put your website there. Even if it's not the home page, put a link to your expert page there. When people want to investigate Workings Moms Only, the first thing they see on my expert page is Mariel Hemingway, which gives me instant credibility. Whatever page you think will generate the biggest "wow," that's the best link to put there. Use this template that I've provided, but tweak it to make it your own voice.

Step 3: Turning Content Providers into Panelists—Abracadabra

Suppose you've sent out the e-mails and gotten some people to respond, but they're not panelists yet. You are just republishing their existing content. After a while, you might wonder, "How do I turn content providers into panelists?"

First, after you run anyone's content, reply with a thank you note and let him know how much your subscribers enjoyed his article by including actual feedback if it's available.

Next, ask for permission to make him a formal panelist so that you can give him a link back to his site. Now he knows he did well and got positive feedback along with additional exposure. This is the time to ask him, "Hey, do you want to get a little more serious? I'd like to put you on my panel. It's such a great fit. You have so much to give. By putting you on my panel, people coming to my site will see the link to your site right underneath your picture and biography."

Don't make content requirements too strict at first. See if he can write just one article a month. When people get a great response to their information, they might even ask, "How much more would you like from me?" At that point, you can say that once a month would be fantastic. This depends on how many subscribers you have and the frequency of your inbox magazine, but saying once a week would absolutely scare that expert away.

Don't ask for more than you can publish. If you are publishing once a week, then getting something once a month from your panelists is just fine. If you publish every day and you have 10 panelists that contribute only once a month, you won't have enough material. Make sure your request for more content is reasonable, but don't ask him to basically write each issue of your inbox magazine.

Don't forget that your panelists get a link back to their site, so you're helping them build their list as well. Also make sure you get permission to republish their old content because many book authors may have contract legalities that won't allow you to copy and publisher entire chapters verbatim. If you have to change an author's content, you want to make sure he knows and approves.

Essentially, you're saying, "I notice you have a stash of articles already written. Would you mind if we edited them and maybe changed a couple of paragraphs so there's no duplicate content issues? Then we'll send it over to you for approval." If you can get permission to do that and still give him author credit, he'll get further exposure without doing any extra work.

"No" Won't Be an Option

Follow these three steps and you'll have almost nobody saying no to helping provide you with the content you need for your inbox magazine. Even if you are brand new and just getting started, you can get people to contribute. When you get big enough, you may even get major celebrities asking to join your panel.

Even better, in the next chapter I'll show you how to create your own content far easier and faster than you might have thought possible. With your own skills and knowledge and the contributions of your expert panelists, you'll never run out of original, useful content that will keep your subscribers happy.

12

You, the Author: Article Writing Made Easy

Your inbox magazine will need content on a regular basis. While you can use outside contributors or panelists to supplement your content, you'll still need to write the majority of the content yourself, especially if your inbox magazine follows the guru model. Writing so much content consistently might sound scary, but there are plenty of ways to make this process a whole lot easier.

The three resources needed for pain-free article writing are:

- Google Alerts
- Voice dictation
- Banked content

Alert Yourself

One of the biggest problems with writing on a regular basis is getting ideas. Everyone can write if you give them a good idea. The hard part is finding that good idea. That's what Google Alerts can give you.

Just visit Google Alerts (www.google.com/alerts), type in keywords related to your topic, and specify the type of information you want and how frequently you want it (see Figure 12.1).

For example, you can tell Google Alerts to send you information posted in the news, on blogs, in video, in discussion forums, or in books. Then you can specify how often you want this information, such as once a week, every day, or as it occurs in real time.

Figure 12.1   Google Alerts makes it easy to get information about certain topics.

Google will e-mail this information to you so that all you need to do is sift through this information, and if it sounds interesting, write about it. It's as simple as that.

Remember, Google Alerts may send you blog posts and articles written by other people. Don't just copy and paste other people's content. That is plagiarism and not the purpose of this exercise. Use Google Alerts to spark your own ideas and help you stay current. Writing about some current event can be hugely important because you'll be providing your subscribers with information based on the news they're already reading about.

Best of all, Google Alerts is not only easy to use, but it is also totally free.

Become a Dictator

This next option is called Copytalk, which is a dictation software service (see Figure 12.2). Many people get intimidated at the thought of writing, but everybody knows how to talk. You can either

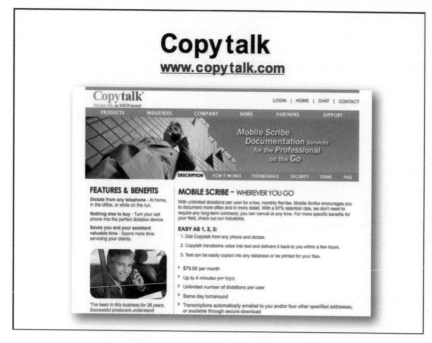

Figure 12.2   Copytalk is a dictation service that converts speech into text.

talk by yourself or interview others. Typically, an article will take you between 4 and 10 minutes a topic, with an average length of 5 or 6 minutes total, depending on how fast you talk and on how many words you say. I typically can talk for 4 minutes to create a 1,400-word essay.

Copytalk lets you send an audio file that they'll transcribe into text and send it right back to you. All you have to do is edit the transcribed text. If you tried to write an article, it might take you an hour, but if you talk for 4 minutes, you can send it to Copytalk and then spend another 20 minutes editing it, so you can complete an article essay in about 25 minutes.

You might have an idea that strikes while you're driving and hear something on the radio. Just turn down the radio, pick up your phone, talk for 4 minutes, and send it off to Copytalk. Before you get home or back to the office, the transcript will be there waiting for you. Copytalk can turn audio into written transcripts incredibly fast. It just doesn't get any easier!

If you have an Apple Macintosh, an iPhone, or an iPad, there's also a built-in dictation feature that works as long as you're connected to the Internet. Just open a word processor such as Word or Pages on your Macintosh, or Pages on your iPad, let the program know you're ready to start dictating, and then talk away.

After every sentence, the program will translate your spoken words into printed text. Such transcription won't always be 100 percent accurate, but it is completely free as long as you're willing to speak a sentence at a time. When you're done, you can go back and edit your transcribed text to correct any omissions or errors, but it will still be far faster than typing an article from scratch.

If you're using a Windows PC, you can always buy voice recognition software such as DragonDictate. Now you'll be able to dictate to your computer and have the software transcribe it into text.

Take It to the Bank

Now let's talk about banking content. This means keeping a reserve of content for each one of your sections within your inbox magazine. I'm going to tell you exactly what I do, but you can do it any way you choose. Remember that you must first define the structure and format of your inbox magazine that lists what sections you have such as an introduction, a main essay, and a "check it out," a "quick tip," and a "look who's talking" section.

Working Moms Only has five sections, so what I do is set up a paper folder for each section. Whenever I come across something relevant, whether it's online, in print, or notes I took down after talking to somebody, I stick it in that folder.

When I need to write something, I go through these folders. Obviously, you can set up folders in your e-mail account and bookmark interesting websites. I like physical folders because I can take them with me and read a lot offline.

If I see something interesting in a book, I can photocopy it, highlight it, and have a physical stack of papers to read when I sit down to write. When you're done with any information, don't throw it away. Move it to a folder for used information because you can always go back and recycle old content but just rewrite it for what's happening right now.

One time I was flying home from New York on Jet Blue airlines. I was watching Dr. Oz on TV talking about the 10 things that women should do every day for better health. I took out my pad and wrote everything down. Then I put these papers in my folders in my briefcase.

It's essentially Dr. Oz's content, but when I went to write my issue, I just added my thoughts on whether this was something I do, something I'm going to start doing, or just how I felt about it. So you get content everywhere. Bank it. Don't try to remember it. Put it somewhere. Put it in your content bank. When it comes time to write your issue, open up your content bank, and your inbox magazine issue will practically write itself.

A lot of creating content involves just thinking differently. You see stuff every day that's interesting and useful and could be talked about. Unfortunately, most of the time you hear or read about it and then forget about it, and it's gone forever. But if you train your brain so that when you see something you think, "Oh, that's good. Now let me bank it," you'll never have to worry about coming up with content again.

For those who prefer storing ideas digitally, there's actually a computer service that works similarly called Evernote. It's basically kind of a computer-based filing system where you can create files that you can tag and label. Just highlight a clump of text on a web page and send it to Evernote. Take a picture with your iPhone and save that to Evernote. Evernote even has an iPhone, iPad, and Android app. If you go to Evernote.com, you can watch their tutorial videos that will show you how to do it.

If I'm ever caught without a paper and pen, I'll always have my iPhone and I'll just type it right in the notes app. So everybody has the resources to bank their content whenever they happen to be.

Creating the Perfect Article Structure Is Golden

Everything you write needs to have one big idea. Too many people write an article with several little ideas, but that never works because you're bombarding the reader with too many different thoughts at once. As a result, they never feel satisfied, but just feel confused instead. You need a single big idea that takes one through the entire essay from start to finish. Such an idea is called a golden thread (see Figure 12.3).

Perfect Article Structure

- Grabbing headline
- Subheadline that details the headline
- Opening paragraph that asks a question
- Big idea that answers the question
- Three supporting bullet points
- Conclusion/call to action

Figure 12.3   Creating the perfect article structure.

Don't try to cover too much information. Start with one big idea and drill down to the details with three supporting bullet points. That's much more compelling.

Start with a headline that grabs you. Why is this important? Because the sole purpose of the headline is to entice someone to keep reading. If you don't have a great headline that grabs, people won't bother reading your content.

The same is true with the subhead. A subhead reiterates why you are reading. When many people write an essay, they just write a long continuous page of text without any subheads to break up their essay. Subheads exist to keep someone interested and excited about the next section.

Your opening paragraph typically needs to ask a question to get the reader involved. Then they'll keep reading to find out the answer to that question.

Finally, conclude with a call to action. Every time someone finishes your article, they should know what to do next. If somebody finishes your article and just thinks that it's interesting but has no idea what to do next, then your article wasn't effective to keep people coming back.

A call to action isn't always telling someone, "Hey, go buy something." A call to action is more like, "Okay, take what you just read and take action to change your life."

If your readers take action on everything that you write, they will read everything you write and love you. That's when you'll become their hero and guru. If they don't take action and find your information useful, then they'll just forget what you wrote and never have a reason to read anything else you might write.

Creating Engaging Content

The content in your inbox magazine, whether it's written by you or by an outside contributor or panelist, should contain at least one of the following elements:

- Be remarkable.
- Be interesting.
- Include statistics people can quote.
- Be funny.
- Simplify complex ideas.
- Evoke emotion.
- Share a secret.

It doesn't matter how well known and creditable an expert might be; if they are giving you boring, tepid content, don't run it. It doesn't matter whose name is at the top. Before you ask somebody to be a panelist, review their writing to make sure that it's exciting and relevant. Make sure they encompass the elements listed above. If they don't, chances are they won't possess those elements when they're writing for you. They must be remarkable.

The literal definition of "remarkable" is anything that's worth talking about. When you write or edit an article, ask yourself if this is something that somebody will want to tell others about.

Even bad stories can be interesting. Bad stories aren't necessarily written poorly. A bad story can be something that doesn't end with an uplifting conclusion.

For example, you might write about the seven copywriting mistakes or marketing blunders. It's the rubbernecker effect where people are fascinated by reading about other people's disasters.

Publish a headline or subject line that says "Bad News" and publish the exact same article with a headline or subject line that says "Good News," and the "Bad News" headline will attract twice as many people just about every time. It's unfortunate, but it's reality.

Remember that people love statistics they can quote. For example, I once wrote an essay for Working Moms Only where I talked about the fact that women who ask for raises will make approximately $500,000 more in their lifetime than women who don't ask for raises. That's a valuable statistic that people can and do remember.

People like to feel smart, which is called the "cocktail talk syndrome." You, as an inbox magazine publisher and author, can help them by providing valuable statistics. Then they can sound smart and interesting, whether they're at a cocktail party or on the golf course, or anywhere in between.

Another example of a statistic that I used in a speech is that for the first time in 2011, there were more women in the workplace than men. Again, that's an interesting fact.

Both of these statistics were perfect fits for my audience. Not only were they interesting but useful and actionable as well.

Another bonding mechanism is to be funny and make people laugh. If you make people laugh and entertain them, they're going to like you, trust you, and read whatever you put out. When you combine information with entertainment, your end result is engagement.

Sometimes being funny often means being self-deprecating. Don't think that you have to put yourself on a pedestal. Make fun of yourself. You want your readers to know that you are human, too. Talk about mistakes that you made. Explain why you made a stupid decision. By admitting your mistakes, you will actually come across as more likable. When I talk about my mistakes, I also explain what I learned and how other people can benefit without making those same mistakes.

Another technique is to simplify complex ideas. The reason why books for Dummies are so popular is that they take complicated ideas and make them easy for anyone to understand.

There's a general rule that you should write to the fifth-grade level, which means that a fifth grader can understand it. The *Wall Street Journal* is actually written to the seventh-grade level, and that covers the complex world of finances and investing.

If you focus your writing to the fifth- or sixth-grade level, your writing will be much more readable. Don't try to impress with complicated words. Simplify. When it comes to writing, never say, "There is a policeman in an automobile," when you can say, "There is a cop in a car."

Most people discuss topics conceptually using complex words. What you want to do is make your topic easy to understand by using shorter words and sentences along with plenty of analogies. For example, you could go into the technical details of how social media networks work, or you could just say that social media networks are like a party.

Twitter and Facebook are like being at a big party where you can meet people, but when you want to start talking about business, then you break off into groups for more privacy and intimacy. At a party, some people might hang out on the back porch, which is like visiting your blog or website.

When you describe social media networks as a party, people can understand what you're talking about right away. Think back to your school days. One of the hallmarks of a good teacher is that they know how to make complex ideas simple.

Whatever you write, you must evoke an emotion to make people relate to you. We all have so much in common that when we get to share a strong emotion we're far more likely to remember the writing and the author. If we aren't moved emotionally, then it's easy to forget what we just read and not even bother remembering who wrote it, either. If you can't move someone emotionally, you're going to have a hard time getting them to take action, which means that subscriber will most likely not buy anything from you either.

Finally, share a secret. Secrets make people feel that you are giving them something they can't get anywhere else. Just think about it for a minute. Who are the people you typically share secrets with? Most likely, they include your best friend, your spouse, a parent, or a sibling. That is the kind of intimacy to strive for with your subscribers.

Before you publish any article for your inbox magazine, make sure it has at least one of these seven elements. If it only has one, it better be really good. Hopefully, it will have a combination of these elements such as being remarkable and funny. If it's not funny, then it needs some rubbernecker information. Does it use statistics? Does it make a complex idea easier to understand? Is it emotional? Does it share a secret?

If an article contains one or more of those elements, then your reader will say, "Wow, I would have never thought of that in a million years. I just got something new here and I can't wait to read the next issue."

Be Remarkable

An inbox magazine isn't about being in the information business. There is plenty of information online already. No one really needs more information. You're really in the opinion, idea, and advice business—because it is your opinion, ideas, and advice that people want!

If all you do is regurgitate existing information, you won't have a reason to exist. You might get some subscribers, but they won't stick around. So don't just regurgitate information because there's no real value added there. Make sure that you're remarkable and interesting, and you'll keep growing your subscriber list with every issue.

13

Sourcing Compiled Content: Done for Your Filler

You can write content yourself, and if you follow the panel model, your panelists can create original content as well. However, sometimes you need filler content for a particular section. That's when you may need go out and source it, even if it's not original.

Compiled content is basically articles published elsewhere that are still relevant to your audience. Unless an article is exceptionally good, you should use compiled content for filler and never for your primary content.

The three main sources for finding compiled content are:

- Private label resale rights (PLR content).
- Article sites.
- Public domain and creative commons sites.

Private Label Resale Content

Private label resale content is best known as PLR. PLR content is basically an article or e-book that someone writes and sells. Anyone buying this PLR article or e-book can now label this article or e-book as their own. The advantage of PLR content is that it can be inexpensive to buy compared to hiring a writer to create something new exclusively for you.

The disadvantage is that because anyone can buy and distribute PLR content, the quality may vary greatly and in many cases, may

Sources of PLR Content

- **EasyPLR.com:** Probably the best quality with selection overall (limited).

- **AllPrivateLabelContent.com:** 100 percent U.S.-written, good quality (limited).

- **ThePLRstore.com:** Dirt cheap PLR, but you have to kiss a lot of frogs (wide open).

- **WarriorForum.com:** Search PLR articles.

- **99centarticles.com:** Get 500-word articles for $5–$7 each (1 hour).

- **ContentDivas.com:** Really high-end custom writing (expensive).

Figure 13.1   Sources of PLR content.

be virtually unusable without additional editing. Be ready to spend a lot of time browsing through PLR content until you find something suitable for your inbox magazine.

The whole point of PLR content is that you can manipulate, modify, and enhance content while claiming credit for it. You don't want to just repurpose somebody else's content. You have full rights to change it however you see fit. You'll want to modify and improve PLR content since anyone else can buy that same PLR content. That's why you don't want to use PLR content without customizing it somehow for your inbox magazine subscribers.

For the most part, PLR content is best as filler content, but you'll need to spend time finding the right PLR content and then even more time modifying it. PLR content can get you started, but you will eventually need to make it your own as well as ensuring that it meets the standards of your inbox magazine.

Still, PLR content can be useful on occasions, so if you want to use it, start with a site like Easy PLR (www.easyplr.com) (see Figure 13.1). Besides using U.S.-based writers for all of their articles, they also limit their membership to reduce the number of people who have access to this library of PLR content. That ensures that many other people can't use the exact same article that you might want to use.

Another place to look for PLR content is the Warrior Forum (www.warriorforum.com). You can search the Warrior Forum for PLR articles and find out what other people have to say about it. If it's not quality content, people will say, "Don't buy this. It was a total waste of money and wasn't original content." If it's good, you'll see people commenting, "This was the best PLR article I've ever seen." People are honest and open on the Warrior Forum.

Two other sources that don't actually offer PLR content but are places where you can pay for custom content are 99centarticles and Content Divas.

The 99centarticles site (www.99centarticles.com) offers original articles for somewhere between $5 and $7 each. This represents an hour's worth of work, but the articles won't be that great and will still require additional editing.

Content Divas (www.contentdivas.com) offers better quality content, but you're going to spend $30 or $40 for each article since it's going to be written by an expert. However, spending $30 to $40 for an article isn't usually necessary unless you are in a real pinch.

Article Sites

One of the best sources of compiled content is EzineArticles.com. With Ezine Articles, you don't have to contact the original authors to get their permission to repost their content. As long as you give them proper credit, you can just grab an article on Ezine Articles, copy and paste it into your inbox magazine, blast it out, and they never have to know about it.

While perfectly legal and ethical, I don't recommend that you do that. Instead, I recommend that you contact them first and ask for their permission. Of course, they are going to say yes because they want the free, additional exposure. Then, later, you can ask them to become a panelist if they're able to provide consistent content on a regular basis that resonates with your readers.

If you have made an effort to contact them and for whatever reason you haven't heard from them, and you want to try something new, take some compiled content from Ezine Articles and run it in your inbox magazine. If you get really good feedback, then contact them again about being a panelist. Only this time you can let them know that their content received positive feedback. Chances are good that they'll respond quickly this time.

Four great article sites are:

- EzineArticles.com
- GoArticles.com
- ArticleCity.com
- WikiHow.com

More often than not, you can rely on these article sites for filler content. Depending on how your inbox magazine is broken up, you might have two articles, so you could use a third-party article for a secondary feature.

If you see an article that you like, especially one on EzineArticles.com, scroll down to the bottom. Below the article you can see the most viewed e-zine articles of the last 60 days and the most published e-zine articles in the last 60 days (see Figure 13.2).

The most viewed articles are the most popular ones people are actually reading online. The most published articles are the ones that other people have posted on their website or in their own inbox magazine. This can be a drawback because it means other people may have already seen this article. However, it also means that the article must be pretty good for so many people to publish it elsewhere.

If you contact the person who wrote one of these more popular articles, you might be able to get her to change the headline or title and tweak the content a bit.

By viewing the article headlines of the most viewed and most published articles, you can see what topics your own audience might like to read.

For example, by viewing the most viewed and most published articles in the financial trading category, you can see article titles on how to become a disciplined trader and why so many traders fail. Now you have a good idea what types of topics might appeal to your own inbox magazine subscribers.

Public Domain Content

The information in this chapter about public domain content is specific to the United States; Europe and Asia have their own laws.

In the United States, any content published before 1923 is in the public domain, which means you can freely copy and use it

If you see an article on EzineArticles.com that you like, scroll down for "Most Viewed" and "Most Published" articles in that category...

Figure 13.2   Finding the most viewed and most published articles on EzineArticles.com.

however you wish. If something was published between 1923 and 1963, but the copyright owner failed to renew it, then that material is also available in the public domain.

Another source of public domain content is anything that the U.S. government creates such as reports or photographs from agencies such as NASA or the Department of the Interior. The taxpayers already paid for it, so it belongs to the public.

Words, names, slogans, and other short phrases can't be copyrighted, which means you're allowed to use quotes from famous people. However, it is possible to trademark a word, a name, or a slogan. Anything trademarked can't be used without written permission.

Some other types of public domain content include blank forms used to record information; calendars, charts, tape measures, and rulers; and recipes. Generally, sifting and finding useful information through public domain content will take some time but may be worth it (see Figure 13.3).

Typically Not Protected By Copyright

1. **All written works by the United States federal government** are in the public domain whether the work is published or unpublished. However, this is not always true of local governments or if the work was created for the federal government by an independent contractor.

2. **Words, names, slogans, and most other short phrases cannot be copyrighted.** This is not, however, to be confused with trademarks.

3. **Blank forms used to record information** are in the public domain.

4. **Works that are common property like calendars, height and weight charts, tape measures, and rulers.**

5. **Recipes.** A list of ingredients is not copyrightable but explanations and notes in a recipe can be.

Figure 13.3   Types of information that is not copyrighted and thus in the public domain.

If you want to give it a try, some great sources for public domain content includes Gutenberg.org, Wikibooks.org, Ibiblio.org, and Scribd. Scribd is essentially an online social media site where you can upload, publish, and share PDF files. People can then download and distribute these PDF files.

To see how you could use Scribd, let's say you want to do an inbox magazine around worm farming because you have a green inbox magazine. First, you'd search for worm farming and then look for the information and rating link (see Figure 13.4).

Clicking on the information and rating link opens a section on the copyright statement. In this case, the copyright is attribution noncommercial, which means you can't sell it, but you can repost the content as long as you give the original author credit (see Figure 13.5).

You can always double check the copyright information by contacting the original author listed on the Scribd site. Then you can contact the author and say, "Hey, I love your composting and worm farming article about nature's recycling system. Is there any way I can republish that in my inbox magazine?"

Now suppose you search for the copyright of a Scribd article and find that it says, "Traditional Copyright; All rights reserved"

Figure 13.4   Searching for copyright information on Scribd.

Figure 13.5   Viewing copyright information for a PDF file posted on Scribd.

"Traditional Copyright": Can't republish it in any way, shape, or form without the author's permission.

Figure 13.6   Some Scribd articles may be fully copyrighted.

(see Figure 13.6). That means you can't do anything with it without written permission, so that information and ratings link is a quick way to find the copyright of a PDF file.

Meat, Vegetables, and Bread

Ultimately, the goal of using any of these compiled content sources is to find panelists for your inbox magazine, not just copy and paste articles.

As the publisher of your inbox magazine, you want to create some original content and rely on your panelists to contribute the majority of your content. Then if you need filler, look for compiled content on article sites, public domain sites, and private label rights sites.

Think of you inbox magazine as a great meal. You are the meat, the main course. Your panelists are the vegetables, a must for good health. And your filler is the bread that you have every once in a while.

CHAPTER

14

Don't Delay: Action You Should Take Right Now

I want you to take action now, so action step 1 is to make a list of the 10 potential panelists for your inbox magazine. You don't have to do this by yourself. Grab a friend, a colleague, or anybody interested in your niche and market, and brainstorm with them. Just start writing any names that come to mind. Afterward, circle the 10 best. That's where you are going to start.

Don't feel like you must be limited to 10. Working Moms Only has 16 panelists because not every panelist will have the time to write something each month. The main reason I want you to choose 10 potential panelists is that if you don't have a specific number to aim for, you'll be less likely to take action.

If you contact 10 people, at least half will likely say yes to you, but there's a good chance that if you ask 10 different people, all 10 of them might say yes. If you ask people the way you've already learned, most people won't say no to anything that promises to give them additional exposure with little or no extra work on their part.

Of course, if you contact 10 people, you may not keep all 10 of those panelists once your inbox magazine starts growing. This will always be an evolving process. Many people who were on the Working Moms Only panel in the beginning are not with me now, and new people have joined. The main point is that you have to start now with at least 10 people in mind, so make that list.

Even if you have people that you may feel you're not quite ready to contact yet, write down their names but put them on another list, not your initial 10 list. These will be people you'll contact once your inbox magazine gets going.

For action step 2, write a template letter that you'll customize for each potential panelist. I gave you a great idea for a letter, but now you have to write your own letter and customize it for your particular market. This should take you 20 minutes at the most. Don't deviate too much from the letter showed earlier. That letter works. You basically just need to customize the letter to make sure the person receiving it knows that you've read their books and are familiar with their work.

For action step 3, you're going to customize each e-mail with each person's name, website, articles, and books you've read. Then define a reasonable time frame to send each e-mail individually. Don't use autoresponders or mass e-mails because that just shows a huge lack of respect.

If someone sees an unsubscribe link at the bottom, meaning that you've broadcasted it, or it's obvious that you bcc'd them because you've included somebody else in the "To" field, people will likely instantly delete your request. Remember, you're just contacting 10 people. That shouldn't take you long to copy, paste, and customize 10 e-mails. Just do it right and you'll get an infinitely better response.

If you are copying and pasting your letters, make sure that you change the names so that you don't call someone by the wrong name, such as calling someone Richard when their first name is Robert. Actually, double check that. You have a potential of ruining a relationship with somebody if you call them by somebody else's name. Double and triple check before you click that send button.

For action step 4, using either compiled content or writing it yourself, collect enough content to publish your inbox magazine for at least two weeks. If you have two issues a week, that's four issues. If you have one issue a week, that's two issues. So you really need to go through that right now and get started.

You may be wondering why you need to do this and not just create them when you need them. The reason is that over the next two weeks, you're going to spend 80 percent of your time getting subscribers and setting up your monetization methods. So you want a head start in creating your content. It takes some extra effort and work, but once you start publishing, you can spend the majority of your time focusing on building your subscriber base, not on worrying about what you are going to put out because you've been so busy setting up your systems and building a subscriber base.

Another reason to create your inbox magazine at least two weeks in advance is if you contact a potential panelist who might say, "I'd love to see an example." If you don't have an example of your inbox magazine ready to show people, you won't be taken seriously.

You don't want to say, "Oh, let me write one and get back to you." You want to say, "Sure, here it is." Make sure that the one issue of your inbox magazine that you use as an example to get panelists is great.

Reality Awaits

At this point, we're moving out of the conceptual, theoretical stage of creating your inbox magazine and moving into the build stage, where we give you the details to create it. You've designed your framework, so now it's time to start building your subscriber base.

Remember, if this is your passion, you're going to love doing this, so get started right now.

PART IV

THE ART AND BRILLIANCE OF A COMMUNITY

It is a critical job of any entrepreneur to maximize creativity, and to build the kind of atmosphere around you that encourages people to have ideas. That means open structures, so that accepted thinking can be challenged.

—Anita Roddick

CHAPTER 15

Landing Pages: Land on It and Squeeze It, Baby

After planning and designing your inbox magazine with expert panelists and your own content, your next question might be, "How do I get subscribers?"

This is where the fun really starts because you can start building your following and have a list of people that you can talk to on a regular basis. If you don't have subscribers, then nobody will read all the great content you've created or compiled. Even worse, without any subscribers, you won't have anyone to pay you money, either.

Up until this point, you've been planning and building your inbox magazine. Now you get to find out who wants to read what you've created. For this, you need to understand the basics of list building, so I'll give you a step-by-step blueprint for getting your first 1,000 subscribers absolutely free.

Quantity Plus Quality Equals a Great List

Of course, there are multiple ways of getting subscribers that involve paying money, but until you have that first batch of subscribers, you won't know the value of your subscribers. You need to know what the average subscriber is worth in the first 30 days and the first 60 days. That way, you'll know how much you can afford to spend to keep growing your community.

On average for a revenue projection, I like to use a metric of 50 cents to $1 per subscriber per month. Of course, this isn't a promise, but it gives you a goal to strive for to identify the value of your own inbox magazine subscribers.

Right now, you're starting from scratch, so you need to learn the basics of list building (see Figure 15.1). You'll need to use and understand the following:

- A landing page
- A lead magnet
- Traffic source

Once you understand the different types of landing pages and the different methods to attract subscribers to your inbox magazine using lead magnets, you'll know how to get your first 1,000 subscribers for free.

Getting those first 1,000 subscribers represents the difference between making money or not. You need to put in work to start an inbox magazine, so you need those 1,000 subscribers to leverage your efforts so you can actually make money. Once you've got that first 1,000, it's easy to jump to 5,000 subscribers, then 10,000, then 15,000, and then 25,000. Breaking that first 1,000 mark represents the key to making money. Once you pass that 1,000 subscriber list mark, you can start earning money that can represent a significant milestone in your life.

You may not necessarily want a half a million or a million subscribers, but you'll probably want 10,000, 20,000, 30,000, or 50,000 subscribers so you can make a good income.

Raw Materials

1. Landing page

2. Lead magnet

3. Traffic source (free/paid)

Figure 15.1   Three steps to getting your first 1,000 subscribers.

As a result, you need to get to 1,000 subscribers as quickly as possible. It's actually possible to do this within the first week, but it's very possible within the first 30 days, so make that your goal.

With Working Moms Only, I reached five thousand subscribers within 24 hours using the methods you're going to learn about in this chapter, and I didn't spend a penny to do it. The goal for the next chapter is to help you get those first 1,000 subscribers without spending any money at all. In order to do this, you need a few items that are easy to create and even easier to duplicate.

First, you need a landing page. A landing page is sometimes known as a "lead capture page" or a "squeeze page," which is a single web page that appears in response to clicking on a search result or an online advertisement. The landing page will usually display directed sales copy that is a synergistic extension of the original advertisement.

Note that a landing page is completely different from the home page of your website. Your website home page is meant to greet people and show them what you have to offer. Although you want to give visitors the option of subscribing to your inbox magazine through your home page, that's not the purpose of a home page.

A landing page's sole purpose is to convince visitors to give you their name and e-mail address, so a landing page is typically much simpler and focused than a home page. A landing page can be just another page on your main website, or it can be a separate domain altogether.

Next, you're going to need a lead magnet. A lead magnet is whatever you choose to give away free in exchange for the information you just requested on your landing page. In most cases, you will be requesting someone's name and e-mail address. Therefore, you need to deliver on your lead magnet by supplying people with something free.

You may be thinking, "Why do I need to offer something? Why can't people just opt in for my inbox magazine?" If you want to build your subscriber list quickly, you need to follow the example of the big traditional magazines.

Think of *Sports Illustrated* giving away football phones to attract subscribers. It's no different for you. You're going to need to give away that extra premium to push people into signing up. Once they sign up with your inbox magazine, your quality and content needs to be good enough to keep them, but you need a lead magnet to get them in the door.

List building is all about having a page where people can opt in and having a lead magnet that compels them to sign up. Then you need to drive traffic to your landing page. That's it. People over-complicate the list-building process, but in the end it's all about traffic and offers.

There are three ways that you can gather subscribers:

- Opt-in form on home web page.
- Pop-up opt-in form on home web page.
- Squeeze or landing page.

The Home Page Opt-in Form

First, you need an opt-in form on your home web page. The absolute best place to put your opt-in form is above the fold and to the right. Above the fold means that your opt-in form should be visible without forcing the reader to scroll down to see it (see Figure 15.2).

Eye-tracking studies have found that most people look on the left-hand side and at the top. Now you may think that you should

Figure 15.2   The opt-in form appears in the upper right corner of the Working Moms Only site.

put your opt-in form on the left-hand side because that's where the eye starts reading. You want your opt-in form to be where the eye stops. In Western cultures, we read left to right. Although we start at the left, we quickly scan past that to end up on the right. Don't alter or change this.

On Working Moms Only, the opt-in form appears with a dominant visual element and an offer to get a complimentary copy of *The Decision Tree* e-book, which is the lead magnet that's emphasized.

Many people do this backwards. Instead of emphasizing the lead magnet to capture someone's interest, they'll promote the complimentary copy of their inbox magazine. Wrong. First, promote the lead magnet. Then mention your inbox magazine.

Every website needs a homepage with an opt-in form in the upper right corner. Here's another example from the Urban Survival Guide website (see Figure 15.3). Besides a professional logo, the opt-in form appears above the fold, which means readers don't need to scroll down to see it. It's right there.

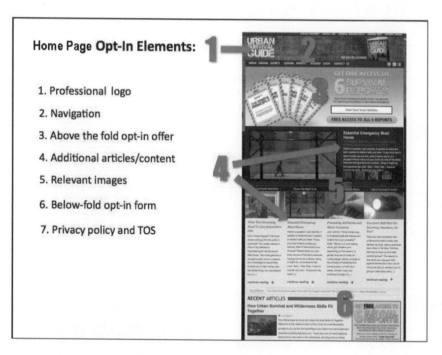

Figure 15.3   The opt-in elements of a typical home page.

Instead of emphasizing the inbox magazine, this opt-in form focuses on the six free survival reports you'll get if you sign up. These six survival reports are the lead magnet. When they sign up, they'll also subscribe to your inbox magazine.

Your website should also include additional articles and relevant images. I also like to have a second opt-in form that's below the fold. Many people will be interested in the content of your site, so they'll scroll down to read it all. Don't make them scroll all the way back up to sign up. That's why you need a second opt-in form below the fold as well.

Don't forget that you'll need a privacy policy and terms of service displayed somewhere on your home page. Eventually, when you start selling your own products, people will want to see your privacy policy and terms of service (TOS). If you ever advertise on Google, Google will want to see this, too.

The Pop-up Opt-in Form

The number two method for getting subscribers is called a pop-up opt-in (see Figure 15.4). The most blatant pop-up opt-in is called a

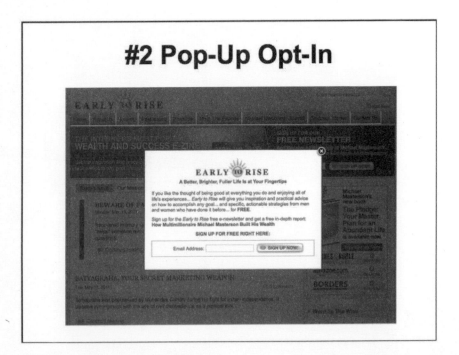

Figure 15.4   A light box pop-up opt-in form.

light box, which grays out the background of your website and pops up right in the middle of the screen.

To create a light box pop-up opt-in form, you don't need to know any type of web page programming. All you have to do is buy it. One company that sells such pop-up opt-in forms is called PopUp Domination. Unlike a lot of pop-up scripts available, PopUp Domination integrates with WordPress and creates absolutely beautiful pop-ups using a template.

This pop-up opt-in form entices people to sign up for the free Early to Rise newsletter and get a free in-depth report on how multimillionaire Michael Masterson built his wealth. Since Early to Rise has been in existence for well over a decade, they have credibility and a brand presence. When just starting out, you should emphasize your lead magnet first and not the newsletter.

Now look at the pop-up opt-in form that the PopUp Domination site uses to advertise their product using a picture of the lead magnet report (see Figure 15.5). If you use PopUp Domination, you'd just have to drop a digital picture of your report into PopUp Domination and the program takes care of showing it properly.

Figure 15.5   A pop-up opt-in form can emphasize the lead magnet as a digital picture.

You may be worried that having pop-ups show up all the time might get obnoxious to your potential subscribers or to your current subscribers. To avoid this problem, you can display them with a timer, such as waiting 30 seconds or 60 seconds. That way people can start reading the content on your site before the pop-up opt-in form appears. You can also track your subscribers with "cookies" so only new visitors see the pop-up opt-in form.

If you don't think your market will like seeing pop-up opt-in forms appear, you can use an alternative option known as a bottom-up opt-in form. When visitors arrive at your site, they'll be able to read the content. Then after a certain amount of time, the bottom-up opt-in form appears (see Figure 15.6).

It doesn't pop up right in the middle, but you definitely notice it. It's not as effective as the light box pop-up, but if you get a lot of complaints or worry that your visitors might dislike pop-up opt-in forms, then try the bottom-up opt-in form.

In this particular example, the bottom-up opt-in form can typically get three to six times the number of opt-ins than from the

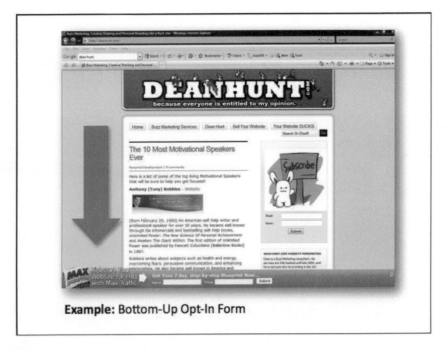

Example: Bottom-Up Opt-In Form

Figure 15.6   A bottom-up opt-in form appears at the bottom of a web page.

standard subscribe box that might appear in the upper right corner of your web page.

Besides delaying the appearance of your opt-in form, you can also define how many times you want this pop-up to appear for each person. For example, you may only want your opt-in form to pop up every five times someone visits your website. That way you're not aggravating them every time they come back to your website.

At the end of the day, you want subscribers. If a couple of people complain, so be it. You're always going to have complainers no matter what you do, so focus on taking actions that will maximize your chance of making money.

If you want to give this option a test, one easy and inexpensive tool to use for bottom-up opt-ins is InstantSlideup (see Figure 15.7).

The Stand-Alone Squeeze Page

By far the best method to attract subscribers is a stand-alone squeeze page (see Figure 15.8). When you send people to a short-form or

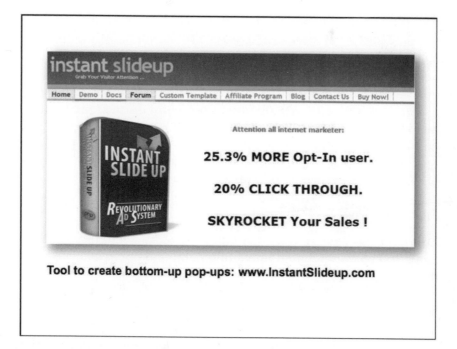

Figure 15.7   Instant Slideup is one of many tools you can buy to create bottom-up opt-in forms.

Figure 15.8   The most effective way to get subscribers is through a squeeze page.

a long-form squeeze page, they have only one choice to make and that's to opt in or not.

Your website can actually offer too many distractions because people can look at past issues of your inbox magazine, see who is on your panel, and browse around your site, reading everything you offer. A squeeze page, on the other hand, serves only one purpose, to get the reader to sign up and subscribe.

Long versus Short Squeeze Pages

A stand-alone squeeze page can still display a logo and information, but is 100 percent focused on getting people to opt in by giving you their name and e-mail address.

An even more effective squeeze page is one that's shorter with no branding whatsoever (see Figure 15.9). The only action you can take is to hit the back button or to subscribe. Depending on where you get traffic, you can use both a short-form squeeze page and a long-form squeeze page.

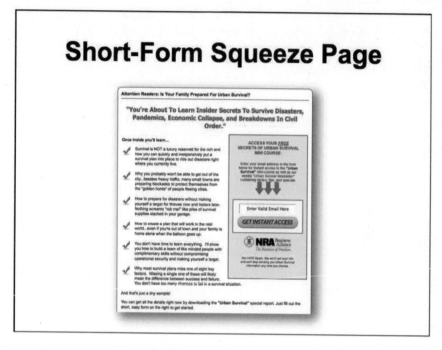

Figure 15.9   A short-form squeeze page.

A long-form squeeze page typically covers several pages, with plenty of chances for the reader to click a button at any time to opt in. Plus, a long-form squeeze page can provide more information and testimonials. As long as people are willing to keep reading, the long-form squeeze page keeps giving them additional information to convince them to sign up.

In comparison, a short-form squeeze page typically appears as a single screen so readers don't have to scroll to see the whole page. At one glance, they can see everything they need to know to either sign up or not.

You can make an even shorter squeeze page that consists of less than a page. Strip away the text until you're left with just your opt-in offer, and now readers have a simple decision. Either they want what you have to offer or not, but those people who do sign up will be the exact type of people you want on your list. You don't want thousands of unqualified people. You want a list that contains nothing but completely qualified people who want what you have.

The short squeeze page shown in Figure 15.10 just makes an offer for free lessons on how to open and run an online store. Readers immediately see a really big promise that follows up with an immediate call to action to enter an e-mail address. Ideally, this squeeze page should also tell people that they'll also be subscribed to an inbox magazine, but that's something that you can easily add later.

As an alternative to displaying large amounts of text, you can also create a squeeze page that consists mostly of video because many people prefer to see an offer rather than read about it. Again, you'll need to test this with your audience and market, but the video basically replaces most of the text while still offering an opt-in form.

A video squeeze page still displays a headline, an opt-in box, a video in lieu of text, and a picture of the lead magnet. Most of the time, a combination of video and text outperforms video alone because the text can entice people to play the video. If you just show a video, people might not know why they should watch the video, so they won't.

Generally, a short-form squeeze page consistently attracts more subscribers than a long-form squeeze page. That being said, when

Learn How to Make Money with an Online Store

Everything you need to know on how to build a niche online ecommerce store from scratch!

- Completely free
- Easy to follow tutorials
- No fluff

Enter your primary email address below and receive a **free** 6 day mini-course via email on **How To Create A Niche Online Store In 5 Easy Steps**

Email Me My Free Lessons To:

Submit

We respect your privacy. Your information will not be shared with any third party and you can unsubscribe at any time.

CREATE A NICHE ONLINE STORE IN 5 EASY STEPS

OPEN

Figure 15.10   A short-form squeeze page can take up less than a page.

you buy advertising such as from Google, they don't want you to direct people to short-form squeeze pages. They'd rather you send people to a branded website with a long-form squeeze page (see Figure 15.11).

A branded squeeze page not only displays your offer, but also displays your company logo so people know the company behind the offer. However, an unbranded squeeze page just promotes the offer but doesn't display the logo of the company behind that offer.

If you are driving traffic from Google, they want to see a long-form squeeze page. Depending on your offer and your market, the long form may outperform the short form, and a branded squeeze page may outperform a nonbranded squeeze page.

However, you always need to test the different variations because one option will never work all the time in all markets. What works most of the time is the unbranded short-form squeeze page, but test it with the other variations to see which one works best for you.

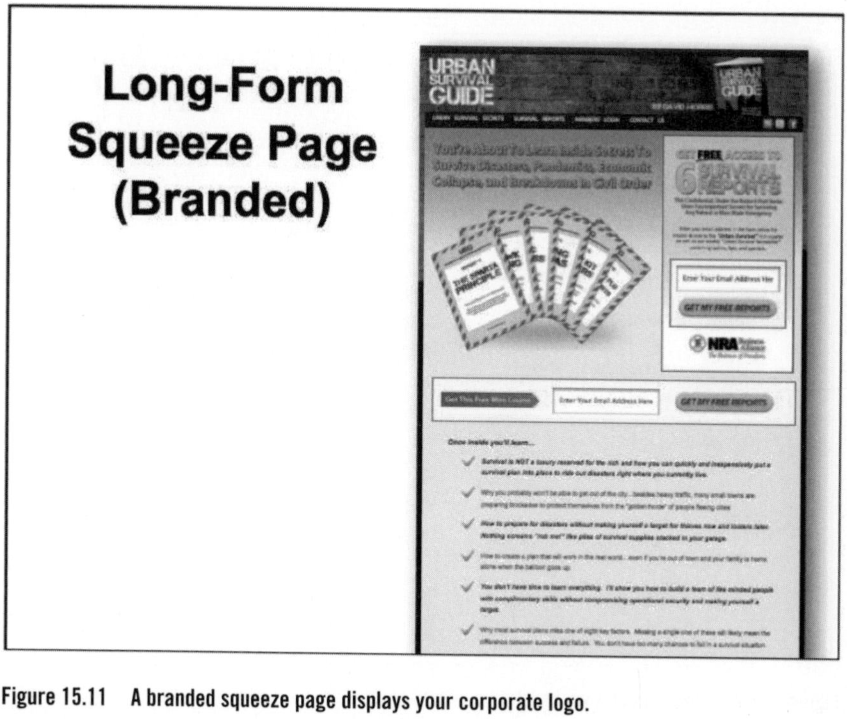

Figure 15.11   A branded squeeze page displays your corporate logo.

The Elements of a Squeeze Page

One important element of a longer-form squeeze page is an attention-getting headline that makes a promise of offering something free or complimentary. I've actually tested the words *complimentary* and *free* and got more responses when advertising something as complimentary instead of free. That's why the squeeze page in Figure 15.12 invites readers to download a complimentary special report.

Next, you need a lead magnet that includes a graphic. Nine times out of ten, showing people a graphical image of what they are going to get, increases your response and gets people to take action and opt in.

Third, you need to display an opt-in form. Most opt-in forms appear vertical in the upper right corner of the web page, but you can also try a horizontal opt-in form that runs across the entire page. There's no chance of missing it because it goes all the way across the page.

Fourth, you need compelling short-form copy that explains your offer in convincing detail. Although large amounts of text can

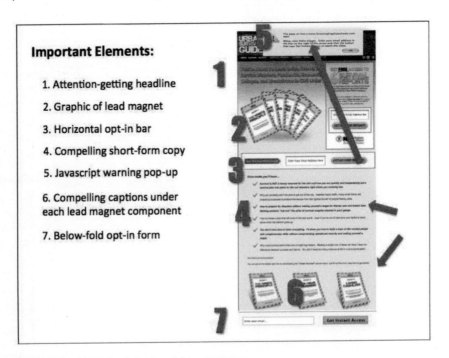

Figure 15.12   Elements of a successful squeeze page.

seem intimidating, if someone's interested in your offer, they can't get enough information to make a decision, so the more information you give them, the better informed they'll feel in taking action to opt in.

Fifth, your squeeze page can display warning pop-ups. For example, you can have an image that appears to offer a video with a play button in it. When people click on it thinking that the video is going to play, the warning pop-up window appears that says, "Please enter your e-mail address in the box to the right of the arrow and click the button that says Get Instant Access to watch this video."

Notice how specific the call to action is: Enter your e-mail address in the box to the right of the arrow and click on the Get Instant Access button to watch the video. That action references the fact that they obviously want to watch this video. It's a good tactic to entice people to opt in.

Aside from your headline, the second most read copy on a squeeze page is the captions. Captions that appear below images are the second most read element after the headline, so you want something that describes what they are getting along with a little bit of a call to action.

Every call to action increases response. Even a little incremental improvement can increase opt-ins by 5 to 10 percent. When you fill a squeeze page with multiple calls to action, three or four times on the page, you can dramatically improve your response rate.

These seemingly minor changes can spell the difference between a 20 or 25 percent conversion rate and a 40 or 45 percent conversion rate. Squeeze pages typically get a 45 or 50 percent conversion rate during an initial launch. These little tweaks that you see in this chapter can get you 40 percent, 45 percent, or even 50 percent conversion rates on a regular basis.

Finally, if you are going to go with a longer-form squeeze page, have an opt-in form at the bottom of your page, so if visitors scroll all the way down, they don't have to scroll all the way back up to opt in. These little details do matter.

When designing the layout of your squeeze page, consider the eye path (see Figure 15.13). People read left to right and down, but your squeeze page should be designed with a specific eye path to make the squeeze page work.

Everybody begins reading in the upper left-hand corner, and that's where they see the various resources available. Then the eye

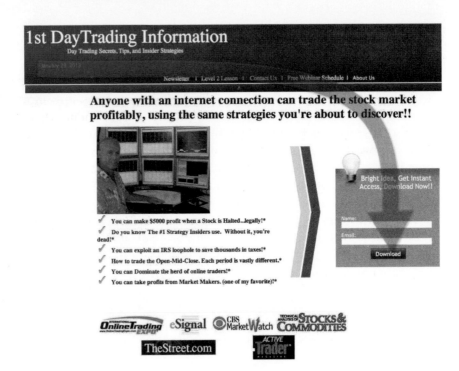

Figure 15.13   Following the eye path of a squeeze page.

goes to the right to see what's going on, and that's when the eye finds the opt-in form where, hopefully, visitors will take action and sign up.

If we don't get them here, the eye path takes them down where there should be a second opt-in form at the bottom of the page. Since you're not asking anyone for money, your opt-in offer can be an impulse move to get your complimentary offer. Don't delay the selling process even though it's free; you're still selling them on giving you good contact info. Let the pictures tell the story.

The eye path needs to lead visitors straight to your opt-in form. Use this model as a starting point. Then test variations for your own market.

Get Out of the Headlights

By now, you should know more about landing pages and how to get subscribers. Think about which options make the most sense for your market. Remember, start with one and get a benchmark. After that, you can test other ideas. So if you think the bottom-up opt-in makes more sense for your potential subscribers than the light box opt-in, go for it. You can always test the light box opt-in later. The same is true with your squeeze page. If you would rather test a short form first because that is what you see mostly in your niche, that's great. Again, once you have a benchmark, you can come back and test your short-form squeeze page against a new long-form squeeze page. The important thing is that you do not vacillate. You need to make a decision, implement it, and track it for results. You cannot be a "deer caught in headlights," not knowing what to do. Any one of the options will work; what you want to find out and find out quickly is which one works best.

In the next chapter, we'll go into much greater depth about lead magnets and their role in getting subscribers.

CHAPTER 16

Lead Magnets: Your Ambassador

Now that you understand how to get subscribers with an opt-in form on a landing page that collects names and e-mail addresses, let's talk about your lead magnet. A lead magnet makes an offer in exchange for someone's giving you his or her name and e-mail address.

In most cases, your lead magnet will be the first piece of content a subscriber receives from you. This is where you need to put your best foot forward and make a great impression. You should think of your lead magnet as the ambassador for your inbox magazine.

The beautiful thing about lead magnets is that you can change them at any time to make sure they stay current and relevant. The more relevant you make it, the better it will serve your subscribers, not to mention increase your conversions as well.

You can have different lead magnets, depending on where you place your offer. If you provide content to a blog targeting working mothers, then your lead magnet might offer a free e-book on how to manage your time. If you provide content to a blog about making money, then you would want a lead magnet that caters to the idea of making more money. The ability to change your lead magnet to target a particular audience is what makes your opt-in offers so flexible.

Think how *Sports Illustrated* markets their magazine. Most people who watch Spike TV are young males, so *Sports Illustrated* might emphasize their swimsuit edition and swimsuit calendar. On ESPN, people are more interested in sports, so they might offer a commemorative Super Bowl football. In the winter, they might offer a fleece pullover. Same idea, different lead magnets. They're just customizing their lead magnet for each particular market and season.

Now you may ask, why use lead magnets? It's because your subscribers want immediate gratification. The job of your inbox magazine is to provide valuable information and maintain a relationship over time. But it may be more difficult to describe the value people will get from your inbox magazine when the issues change from week to week and month to month. At Early to Rise, which targeted entrepreneurs, one issue might focus on improving productivity and another issue might focus on ideas for making money.

So you have to give them the immediate gratification by giving people a compelling reason why that offers an immediate promise and benefit. More important, when people request your lead magnet, make sure you tell them that they'll be signing up to your inbox magazine at the same time (see Figure 16.1).

You may be proud of your inbox magazine, but don't pontificate on its greatness since they can't experience the value yet. Let your inbox magazine do the talking once you have them on your list. For now, just focus on the lead magnet and deemphasize your inbox magazine.

Figure 16.1   A lead magnet gets people to opt in to your inbox magazine.

Types of Lead Magnets

A lead magnet can be a digital product or a physical product. Examples of a digital product include reports delivered as a PDF file or audio stored as an mp3 file. A physical product could be a CD or DVD if you want to ship something.

The Reciprocal

When you send a digital product, you only need a person's e-mail address. However, if you need to ship a physical product, you need a person's full contact information, which can be useful for your particular market later on. But here is the catch: the more information you ask for from someone, the lower your conversions will be. So to start, I recommend using a digital product as your lead magnet.

Generally, people don't listen or watch an audio or video file as much as they read a report stored as a PDF file. Even better, it's easy for someone to share a PDF file by e-mail. It's more cumbersome to share a big mp3 file and even harder to share a big video file. People can always forward download links to audio or video files, but PDFs just get passed along more. Plus, they have a higher perceived value.

You need to promote your lead magnet as a special or secret report that's hot off the press. When you do this, subscribers are more likely to read it. And that is what you want—consumption from your subscribers. This is how you turn your subscribers into readers, your readers into fans, and your fans into advocates. If they do not consume your lead magnet, they can never be your advocates.

Digital products are also simpler from a business perspective. Not only are digital products easier to send, but people get them instantly with no extra shipping or storage issues on your part.

Sometimes you can even use a squeeze page that doesn't offer a lead magnet at all. Such an ultra-short-form squeeze page consists of nothing but a headline, an opt-in box, and a button that represents the call to action. Sometimes this call to action reveals a big secret or promises an easy tip.

In the example shown in Figure 16.2, the reader is intrigued by the question of "How Did This Investor Pocket $1,000,000,000 in One Day?" Of course, when people sign up to get the answer, they also agree to a free subscription to Dr. Martin Weiss's Money and Markets inbox magazine for financial news and investment picks. This ridiculously simple tactic sends all these people opting in straight to reading a much longer sales letter.

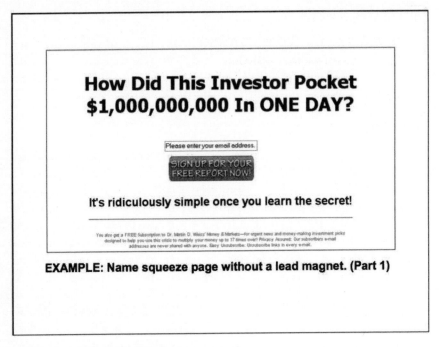

Figure 16.2   A squeeze page with no lead magnet.

This squeeze page doesn't promise any content and none was delivered. Following the opt-in, people get directed to a sales letter that delivers on the squeeze page's promise on how an investor, named George Soros, pocketed a billion dollars in a day.

If your primary goal is to get subscribers to your inbox magazine, this type of squeeze page followed by a sales letter can be aggressive. However, if you are purchasing media to build your list, this method can help you recoup your investment faster. You can also send this method to your current list of subscribers to convert them into buyers.

Not Peanut Butter and Jelly

Another model, called the sandwich content, accomplishes the same speed of monetization, but inserts a little bit of content so it doesn't feel quite as aggressive (see Figure 16.3).

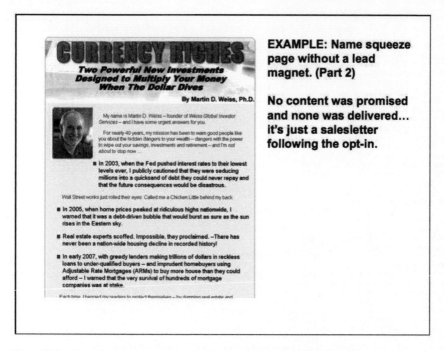

Figure 16.3   The sales letter that appears after people opt in on the squeeze page.

A traditional lead magnet entices readers to give their name and e-mail address in return for something valuable. If you omit a lead magnet and direct people straight to a sales letter, that might feel too aggressive and actually drive people away. The compromise is the sandwich page.

First, you offer people really useful information, but without derailing the sales process. The sandwich page is a small, easily consumed piece of content sandwiched between the opt-in page and your sales page.

While a traditional lead magnet might be a PDF file containing several pages, a sandwich page typically provides much shorter and simpler information that people can understand at a glance. On Working Moms Only, I offer a simple chart called "The Success Indicator" (see Figure 16.4). By looking at this chart, people can quickly see the traits of successful people and unsuccessful people.

Figure 16.4   A sandwich page can offer simpler content.

The content on a sandwich page is meant to deliver on your promise while being quick and easy to understand. In the example shown in Figure 16.5, the opt-in page displays a headline that teaches guys how to tell when a woman's ready to be kissed. Just use your first name and a valid e-mail address as your password. Then click the free instant access button. You aren't actually subscribing. Your e-mail address is just your password.

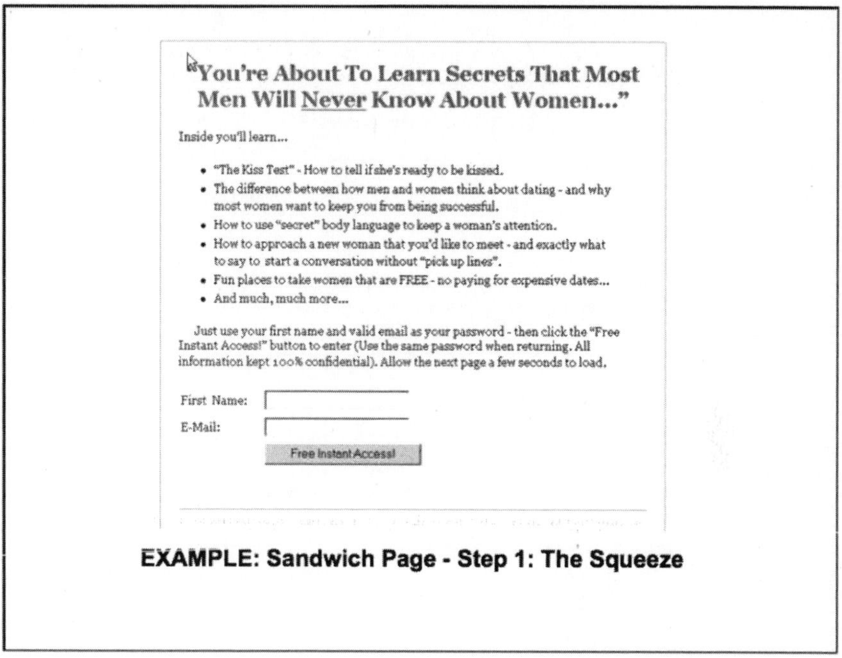

EXAMPLE: Sandwich Page - Step 1: The Squeeze

Figure 16.5   The first part of the sandwich page captures a name and e-mail address.

What happens after he gets their information? Does he send them to download a report stored as a PDF file? Does he send them to a blog with a bunch of articles? Does he just add them to a list to contact them again in the future? Nope. He gives them their promised content about the kiss test. It's six paragraphs that can literally be consumed in a minute or two. Then you have a link here to the next page (see Figure 16.6).

So you consume the content, right? He has fulfilled on the promise and offered a good initial first transaction. It doesn't matter that it wasn't a 50-page PDF report. You want quality, not quantity.

Notice that at the end of the page, it doesn't say, "Click here to buy something." It's just says, "Next page." So I just consumed some content and it was good. When I click "Next page," what am I thinking I'm going to get? More content.

I'm thinking about those other promised benefits back in those bullet points: the kiss test, the difference between men and women, secret body language, how to approach without pickup lines, best

"How To Tell If She's Ready To Be Kissed"

I used to have no idea if a woman was ready to be kissed.

I could be sitting there talking to her, thinking to myself "Wow, her lips really look nice..." but I didn't know what to do next. This would often leave me kissless, and many times kissless for good, as I didn't get another chance.

Here's what I do now:

If I've been talking to a girl, and I want to know if she's ready to be kissed, I'll reach over and touch her hair while we're talking and make a comment about it. I'll say "Your hair looks so soft" and just touch the tips of it.

If she smiles and likes this, I'll reach back over and start stroking it again, but this time I also glance down at her lips and back up to her eyes a couple of times. If she lets me keep touching her hair, I know that she's ready to be kissed.

By using "The Kiss Test" I've been kind and complimentary, but by being very SUBTLE about it, I haven't given her anything she can object to. I now have a way of knowing if she's ready to be kissed that NEVER gets me rejected—and I know within 5 minutes what it used to take me hours or days to figure out...

Next Page

EXAMPLE: Sandwich Page - Step 2: The Content

Figure 16.6   The second part of the sandwich page provides the promised content.

places, and so on. Now I'm thinking that I'll get all that on the next page. Then the sales letter appears (see Figure 16.7).

A sandwich page needs to be consumed in one sitting, preferably in less than five minutes. When a sandwich page takes people to the sales page, they're already primed to receive more content, so they'll be more likely to buy whatever you have to offer. Sandwich pages can double your conversions, which means you can make twice as much money while building your list faster.

You can experiment with different types of squeeze pages at the same time or at different times, so don't think you have to do one or the other. You can combine them or use them independently.

Be a Leader with Your Lead Magnet

Remember, your lead magnet is going to be one of the first pieces of content that your subscriber consumes from you. And the one thing all lead magnets have in common is that they can make you or break you. All of the types of lead magnets work with the right

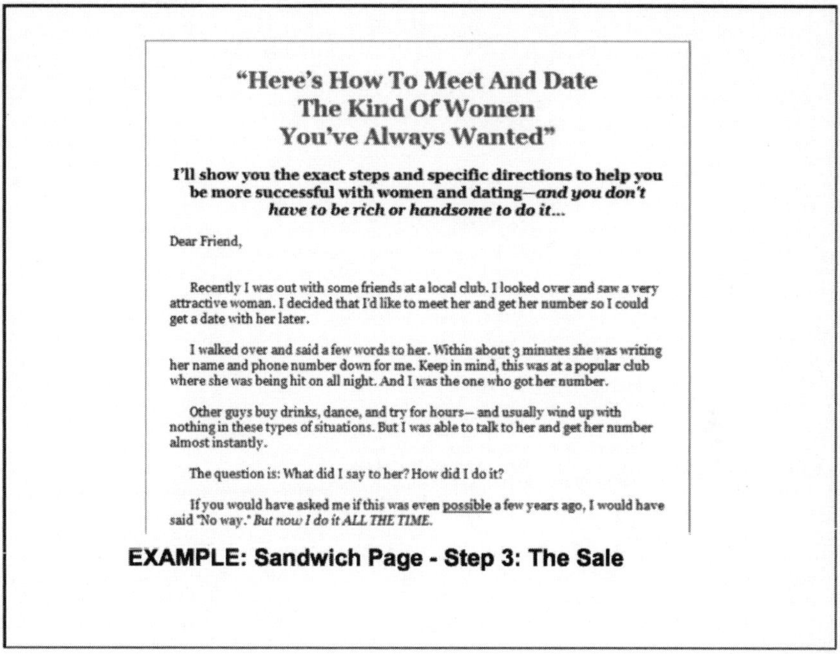

**"Here's How To Meet And Date
The Kind Of Women
You've Always Wanted"**

I'll show you the exact steps and specific directions to help you
be more successful with women and dating—*and you don't
have to be rich or handsome to do it...*

Dear Friend,

Recently I was out with some friends at a local club. I looked over and saw a very attractive woman. I decided that I'd like to meet her and get her number so I could get a date with her later.

I walked over and said a few words to her. Within about 3 minutes she was writing her name and phone number down for me. Keep in mind, this was at a popular club where she was being hit on all night. And I was the one who got her number.

Other guys buy drinks, dance, and try for hours— and usually wind up with nothing in these types of situations. But I was able to talk to her and get her number almost instantly.

The question is: What did I say to her? How did I do it?

If you would have asked me if this was even <u>possible</u> a few years ago, I would have said "No way." *But now I do it ALL THE TIME.*

EXAMPLE: Sandwich Page - Step 3: The Sale

Figure 16.7   The third part of the sandwich page offers a product to buy.

content, and they will also fail if you do not put your heart and soul into it.

So just like your opt-in forms and squeeze page, decide which type of lead magnet is best for your market and give it its best possible chance of success by overdelivering on the content.

Now that you have a good understanding of both lead magnets and landing pages, it's time to talk traffic in the next chapter. Specifically, you'll learn how to get those first 1,000 subscribers.

Your First 1,000: It's a Numbers Game

Once you've got your web page set up and all three subscription methods in place (your home page opt-in, your pop-up opt-in, and your stand-alone squeeze pages), you'll need to test and see what works best. When you've got your lead magnets in place, you're ready to start taking on traffic and building your subscriber list.

Ideally, you want to get your first 1,000 subscribers without having to spend a penny. Getting your first 1,000 subscribers will be the most difficult mission of your entire inbox magazine, especially when it's brand new. But the good news is that once you have the first 1,000 subscribers, going from 1,000 to 5,000 and then to 10,000 is much easier and usually happens even faster. That's because once you have that first 1,000, you'll have useful data that tells you what worked and what didn't work. Plus, you should also have money coming in from those first 1,000 that you can spend on advertising to help you build your list.

There are six easy steps to get you started:

Step 1: Social media marketing

Step 2: Article marketing

Step 3: Active content syndication

Step 4: Press releases

Step 5: Viral PDFs/infographics

Step 6: Ad and resource swaps

All of these are really good methods for publicizing your inbox magazine and getting subscribers to opt in with their name and e-mail address. Of course, some of these methods will be easier for you than others, depending on the market you're in and the assets you already have. You don't necessarily have to do all of them, but the more you can do, the faster you will get your first 1,000 subscribers.

Step 1: Social Media Marketing

Always go after the low-hanging fruits. That means do the easy things first, see what happens, and act and react quickly. Remember, in today's age of social media, everything happens much faster in business than it did 10 years ago, 5 years ago, 2 years ago, or even 6 months ago. Use this to your advantage and ride that wave hard and fast.

Start by tweeting on Twitter and posting all your new issues. As soon as a new inbox magazine issue is ready to go, you need to tweet and post them all. Then you need to encourage people to retweet them.

Once they do, you have to keep that conversation going. You're not just going to say, "Oh, please retweet this to your list." You want to thank the person who tweeted and add more to the conversation, such as asking them what they liked about that particular issue. Keep the conversation going by being engaged, interesting, and informative. The more you participate, the more people are going to retweet it for you.

If you don't know how to do that, you just simply put the @ symbol with their Twitter user name and then just say, "Thanks so much for the retweet. Tell me what else you would like to learn about." They might come back and say, "You're welcome. I would love to learn about organic gardening." Now there's more conversation going on about your particular issue, driving folks back to your web page where they can read the issue and, more important, subscribe to become a part of your ongoing community.

Many people think that they don't need to tweet anymore if they have a Facebook page, but when I tweet my issues, all kinds of people retweet them. These people range from my own expert panelists like Mariel Hemingway to followers in different countries around the world. There is tremendous reward with very little effort with Twitter.

Best of all, the two are not mutually exclusive. You need to do both Twitter and Facebook. Mention every issue of your inbox magazine on Facebook and post at least a summary of each issue on Facebook. It's just another way for your content that you're already creating to go viral inside of a social media platform.

Make sure you add Like and Share buttons to all of your web pages, along with adding Facebook comments (see Figure 17.1). Comments are great social proof, but they don't go as viral. People aren't commenting on blogs as much because they have to keep going back to the blog. People can make Facebook comments right on your page, but unlike a normal blog comment that only shows up on your website, a Facebook comment shows up on your website and your Facebook newsfeed. So everybody associated with it sees it.

Now if someone left a Facebook comment about Working Moms Only, there's a good chance that their friends on Facebook, who might also be working moms, might be interested. If someone says, "Wow, MaryEllen, I loved your latest issue of Working Moms Only." Then one of their friends sees that and wonders "What's this Working Moms Only thing?"

Figure 17.1   Put social media icons in your inbox magazine pages.

Not only is this conversation happening on your site, but it's happening on all these other people's Facebook feeds. So all these people's friends are watching this conversation happen live and in real time. That's why having Facebook comments on your site is a good way to keep people interested.

Add Facebook comments to your web page and add your social buttons to all your e-mail issues (see Figure 17.2). Now people can follow you on Twitter, find you on Facebook, and share your e-mail with others. If you put your social media links at the top of your web page instead of the bottom, more people will see it and be more likely to share it.

Set up a dedicated Facebook page for your inbox magazine and encourage comments and discussions to create viral traffic. If you're not on Facebook, you should be. Even if you don't like it that much, it matters, and if you're not on Facebook, you're going to fall behind.

It's not just about having your own personal profile on Facebook. You also need to have your own Facebook page for your inbox magazine. Start with your own Facebook page to showcase your content and drive people to become fans of you and your page.

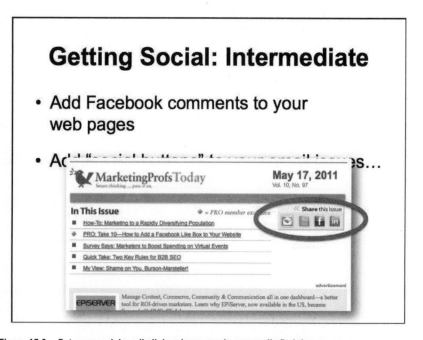

Figure 17.2   Put your social media links where people can easily find them.

At the end of each issue of your inbox magazine, encourage your readers to comment on your Facebook page. Instead of sending them back to your blog or home page to comment, send them to a Facebook page, whether it's your page or a specific fan page to your inbox magazine.

In the beginning, build your Facebook page around you. Post a snippet of an issue and get people to start talking back. Facebook is much more viral than blogs and has far more users.

When someone comments on an issue, ask them what they would like to see in an upcoming issue? It's a great place to get ideas. Ask people what experts they would like to hear from?

If you have a respectable Twitter or Facebook following right now, that should be enough to get you at least 250 subscribers. It's possible you could get your first 1,000 subscribers just by reaching out to your social media following.

Of course, there are many other social media outlets. However, the goal of this chapter is to introduce you to the ones that will get you the most subscribers the fastest. So start with Twitter and Facebook, and learn the other five tactics in this chapter. You can go after more "social media networks" later.

Step 2: Article Marketing

Article marketing is about leveraging content you already have. Just remember, leverage equals dollars. Articles can increase traffic to your site with the potential that one of your articles could go viral at any time.

When I worked at Early to Rise, we ran an article on breast cancer during National Breast Cancer Awareness Month. Not surprisingly, that article got picked up by a major consumer health journal, and that brought in an additional 10,000 subscribers from that one issue alone. Keep in mind that this article was written by an esteemed medical doctor who was one of our panelists. I share this with you so you can see how everything we have discussed thus far ties together.

Someone who reads your article and signs up for your inbox magazine is already interested in your topic. You can't ask for a higher-quality subscriber than that. Subscribers you get through social media friends may give you quantity, but article writing can give you quantity with high quality as well.

Having your articles published on other sites positions you as an expert in your market quickly. The faster that happens, the faster more people will want to work with you. Best of all, article writing is free.

There are two ways articles can generate traffic and subscribers (see Figure 17.3). First, post your articles on different article directories such as EzineArticles.com and GoArticles.com. Now your article gets traffic from the search engines finding it on those article sites. A more indirect method involves somebody's visiting one of these article sites and publishing your content in their own inbox magazine in the same fashion that you could do.

If you have real content, the search engines will find you. For example, a gentleman named Harold Hsu published an article on EzineArticles.com called "Forex Hedging Systems: Are They Useful?" He had a compelling title and useful information, so it got ranked on Google (see Figure 17.4). When someone searches for "Forex hedging systems," they'll see his article, read it, and see his resource box where they can get more information about Harold and anything else he sells.

If you just post an article on an article depository site, people will still likely find and read it, but here's the secret. At the bottom of every article you write (along with the bottom of your website and inside every inbox magazine you send out), put a little blurb about your inbox magazine to drive people to sign up for it (see Figure 17.5). If they liked your article, they'll be motivated to check out your website and inbox magazine, too.

How It Works

Two primary ways you can use articles to generate traffic:

- **The direct method:** Your content gets indexed by search engines such as Google and Yahoo so that YOUR ARTICLES appear anytime someone searches a phrase related to your article topic.

- **The indirect method:** Your content gets "picked up" by newsletter publishers and website owners and is then syndicated to their subscribers/visitors.

Figure 17.3   How article writing can reach people.

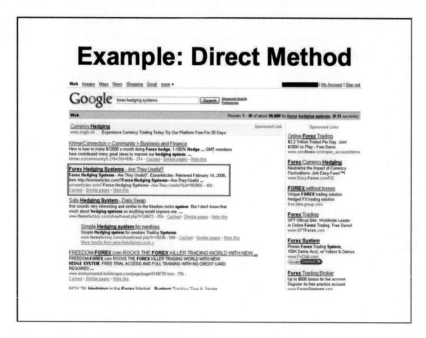

Figure 17.4   Search engines can find your article for others to read.

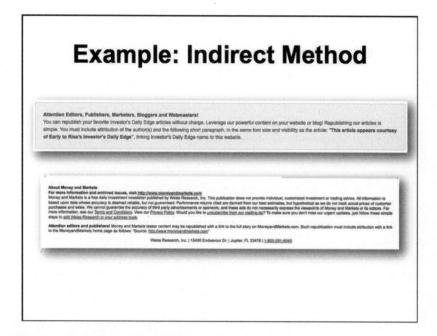

Figure 17.5   Publicize your site and inbox magazine at the bottom of every article.

If you write a great article, let any editor, publisher, blogger, or webmaster repost it freely and easily. Not every article you write will get republished, but if it just happens once, it could mean hundreds, thousands, or even tens of thousands of subscribers.

Here are the components of a winning content syndication strategy:

- A keyword relevant title.
- Great content.
- A resource box with a compelling call to action.

A keyword relevant title helps search engines find and rank your article. Tweak your article titles to make them more keyword rich. The title needs to suggest a specific benefit for the reader.

For example, you saw the earlier article title about forex hedging systems. But the title wasn't just about forex hedging systems; it was about why forex hedging systems are good. The title catches your eye because it asks a question: "Forex Hedging Systems: Are They Useful?" Questions are good just as long as the article delivers on the title.

Don't worry about the length of your titles. You can use up to 100 characters if you want. Here's a good formula to follow:

Keyword Phrase—Benefit-Rich or Attention-Getting Title

Let's say you're trying to get ranked for the keyword phrase "forex trend trading." To do this, you might create a title like this: "Five Tips for Catching Every Trend."

That title contains a hook that promises a specific benefit. To further leverage this content, you could add, "Forex Trend Trading—Five Tips for Catching Every Trend."

Now you've got "Forex Trend Trading" along with another keyword, *trend*, in the end. The first part of the title is to grab the attention of the search engines. The second part of the title is to grab the attention of people. The first part of the title will get it ranked by the search engines, but the second part is what will entice people to read it. Sometimes creating a title can be as simple as just slapping whatever keyword you want at the front and adding whatever keyword you want at the end.

For Working Moms Only, I could create a title that was "Five Tips for Raising Compassionate Children"; then I might include additional words up front to catch the search engines like this: "Busy Working Moms—Five Tips for Raising Compassionate Children."

If you publish an article, make sure that article can get linked by the search engines to help people find it. To improve your chances of being seen, you can also republish the same article with a few modifications. If somebody gives me content for Working Moms Only that she's already published elsewhere, I ask her to change at least the first two paragraphs. This lets her customize the article to my target audience while also providing unique content.

I like breaking up articles into chunks with bullets, numbered lists, and subheads that contain a couple of relevant keywords. As a general rule of thumb, don't write more than five sentences per paragraph to make your text easier to read.

Finally, look at the way your article ends (see Figure 17.6). You could have a hard or soft ending. A hard ending abruptly ends, and then the next thing you see is the resource box that provides links for how to get more information about the author.

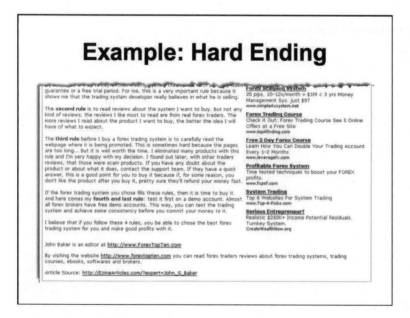

Figure 17.6   A hard ending ends the article without any transitions.

A better way to do it is to include a last paragraph that summarizes the article and invites the reader to learn more by contacting the author to download a free report of some kind.

Can you see how the soft ending just flowed naturally into the resource box as opposed to the hard ending that just stops (see Figure 17.7). When people see a hard ending, they just say, "Oh, the content is over, the article is done." With a soft ending, people will generally keep reading and want to click on the additional links to learn more.

See how the title, content, and resource box come together in a systematic way? The most important part of the content body is to flow directly into the resource box.

Many people wonder if they need a resource box at the end of any article that they post on their own website or inbox magazine. No. Have a call to action to send them off to buy a product, but if they're already on your site or they've already subscribed to your inbox magazine, you don't need to get them to subscribe again.

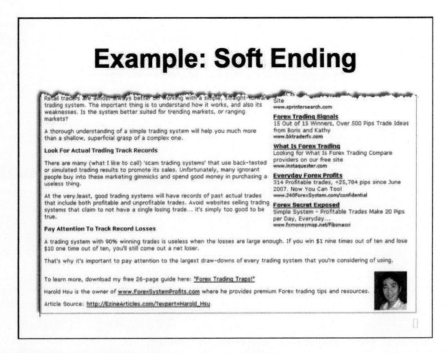

Figure 17.7   A soft ending invites people to contact the author.

Now let's talk more about that resource box (see Figure 17.8). Use connector phrases instead of just listing your name. Your name should go at the bottom of the resource box, not the top. If you insert a picture in the resource box, put a picture of your lead magnet instead of your face. This is not the place to list your accolades. This is the place to let the reader know you have more useful, actionable advice for them free, which is, of course, your lead magnet.

With connector phrases, you entice the reader to learn more. Don't talk about you and don't talk about your inbox magazine. Emphasize the lead magnet. When doing so, make sure you use one absolute URL, and one or two anchor text URLs.

What do I mean by that?

Whenever you see something that begins with "http://www," that's an absolute URL. You want an absolute URL because if somebody just copies and sends it out, the absolute URL will become a clickable link.

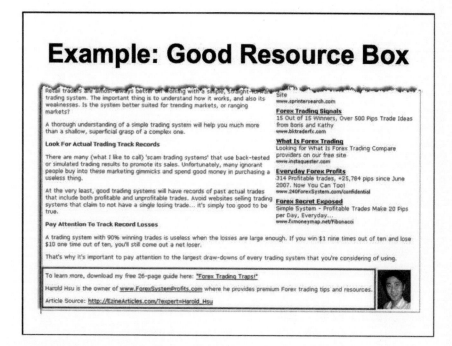

Figure 17.8   An absolute URL creates a clickable link.

Anchor text URLs are links that appear as text. If someone copies and pastes an anchor text URL, those links will not be clickable automatically.

The advantage is that anchor text URLs let you add more keyword phrases. You don't want only anchor text URLs because you can't share the link (see Figure 17.9), so the rule is definitely to have one absolute URL and one or two anchor text URLs.

Most article syndication sites will limit you to two or three links in your resource box. If you only get two, make one an absolute URL and the other an anchor text URL. If you have three, then you can have two absolute URLs.

When it comes to the article submission itself, submit your articles to the following sites:

- EzineArticles.com
- GoArticles.com
- ArticleCity.com

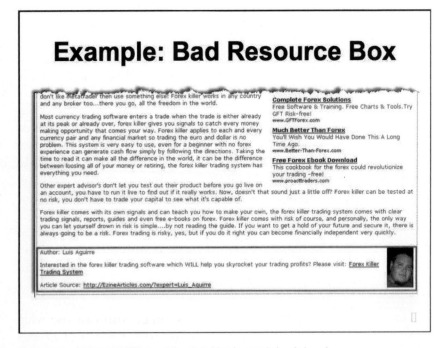

Figure 17.9   Anchor text URLs can't be clickable when copied and shared.

- iSnare.com
- ArticleAlley.com
- SearchWarp.com

Ezine Articles, GoArticles, and Article City are the three biggest ones. Be careful about services and software that claim to automate your submission to hundreds of sites automatically for one low price. The better article sites, such as Ezine Articles, won't accept any submission unless you do it yourself. Also, make sure that you post your articles at EzineArticles.com first since they won't approve an article if it has already been posted on another article site.

That's why you may need to change the title and those first hundred characters to make your article substantially different to avoid duplicate content issues. If you published an article in your inbox magazine, you could still submit it to Ezine Articles and then post it to your site. Take care of your subscribers first and post it to your site.

Don't worry about duplicate content posting the same article to all these different sites. Content syndication is the way the web works. When search engines like Google, Bing, and Yahoo! detect the same content appearing multiple times for the same search phrase, they'll list only one site, whether it's Ezine Articles or GoArticles, or Article City, or your own site, that it deems has the highest authority based on the page ranking.

If you are thinking that you need to create custom articles for all six directories, stop right there. You don't. You don't want or need to modify the same content six different times because the return on your time is not worth it. Just post the same content to all six article sites and let them fight it out for the highest ranking. The person who is going to subscribe is the person who reads your article regardless of where they read it.

If you're still worried about the duplicate content and want to make sure that the content on your site is unique, you can use a service called Copyscape.com. Copyscape searches the Internet for duplicate content, but it's not something most people worry about.

By following this article marketing strategy, you can use what you already have without a whole lot of extra work and greatly increase your exposure to attract more subscribers.

Step 3: Active Content Syndication

In the previous step about article marketing, you learned how to syndicate your content all over the Internet in hopes that somebody will come along, pick it up, and run it. It's a great strategy that you need to do because it does work. However, you don't only want to do something and then hope and pray. You want to actively make the cash register ring. That's what proactive content syndication is all about.

Content syndication basically means taking content that you've previously written and doing the panel model in reverse. Instead of looking for people to be on your panel, you want to proactively get on other people's panels.

Start with the inventory of your competitors that you read every day. The bottom line is that your inventory of competitors needs to be synergistic so that it's a good fit for your community because you're the advocate for those people.

Becoming a panelist for another inbox magazine is a great option. However, you can also be a guest blogger or an official contributor in association and trade journals (see Figure 17.10).

Figure 17.10   Becoming a panelist on other people's inbox magazines increases your exposure.

Your goal is to become a regular contributor in whatever media will give you exposure and bring you the names. Remember to think out of the box because leverage equals money.

I do the exact same thing with my Working Moms Only content. For example, I'm also a panelist on The Balancing Act. I write an issue on Monday, and it's published on The Balancing Act's website on Wednesday. Same exact content. How easy is that? The only difference is the resource box at the end goes to a squeeze page to get my free report, which is my lead magnet. I also have a tracking link so I know where my new subscribers are coming from.

Don't think that you can't do this because you're not a world-renowned expert. Everybody wants and needs good content. If you have quality information and advice, somebody will want your content even if you're not a celebrity.

Making Contact

So how do you contact people to be a panelist or guest contributor? Personalize an e-mail message by complimenting their newsletter, blog, or website. Reference a mutual friend or colleague if possible since that sets the stage nicely.

Then put a link to your site and the specific content that you'd like them to post. That's important so they can see your information with as little effort as possible. Don't make them do the work. If you make somebody else work, they probably won't do it and nothing is going to happen.

Tweak your article to make it match their tone and content. If their site is more formal or serious, then you have to be more formal or serious. Find out how long their articles typically run, such as between 500 and 750 words or more than 1,000 words. Match your content to types of content they're already publishing. If someone sees your article and sees that they'll just have to copy and paste it, your chances of getting accepted is infinitely greater than if it's not quite long enough or the tone isn't quite right.

Figure 17.11 is an example of an e-mail that I received. Study how the writer first introduced herself through a mutual acquaintance and continues to emphasize if there's anything she can do for me, not constantly asking for what I can do for her.

Well, how synergistic is that with Working Moms Only? She listed her website link so I could click on it without doing any

Script example (actual e-mail)

Hi Mary Ellen,

Joe Smith is a friend of mine and contacted me about making a connection with you, as he thought we should meet. If I can ever contribute content for you or be of service in any way, please let me know.

I am CEO of Superwoman Lifestyle which is a movement, community and coaching
practice for women entrepreneurs where I teach them how to live their life in Business, Beauty and Balance so that they CAN have it all.

If you feel I can be of value or service, please let me know, my web site is www.vickiirvin.com

I love your story and all you have done, I have seen you speak for Dan Kennedy and Bill Glazer and heard great things about your business building skills! Impressive and I love how all the men are looking to YOU for your expertise!!!

Thanks!
Vicki Irvin

Figure 17.11   An example e-mail message for contacting inbox magazine publishers.

searching. The only thing I might add would be including a link to an article on her website.

As you can see, her tone was friendly and engaging. So be positive. Be upbeat. People want to help other people who have something good going on. No one wants to work with a downer.

Step 4: Press Releases

What you need to know about the media is to give them what they want. The media is looking for news about subjects their readers are already interested in. You have to capture their readers' interest, and you do that by understanding who their readers are.

Next, give the media captivating and curious tidbits. Often, the press needs filler content like top 10 lists or results from a survey that are interesting and relevant.

It's easy to take articles you've already written for your inbox magazine and convert them into a press release. Just spin it a little bit differently so it sounds interesting to the readers and sounds a little more formal. The number one factor is your title. Use brand names in your title.

If your press release (PR) comes and has an attention-grabbing title and headline, and you can incorporate a brand name or something current in the news, that's going to be even better.

I have a friend who released a muscle-toning product for women's arms. He wrote the PR that just described the product and how it could shape your arms. I told him to change the title to "Get Michelle Obama's Arms" because when she became the First Lady, everybody was talking about her arms. It was the exact same information in the original PR, but the timing, relevancy, and attention-grabbing title made the PR more attractive.

With PRs, use the 80/20 rule. That means focus 80 percent of your PR energy and resources on 20 percent of the media market that you know will work.

Target a specific audience. A PR for Working Moms Only certainly wouldn't target lumberjacks no matter how many of them I could reach.

Find out what kind of stories your targeted media seems to enjoy. Then create a story that interests them and ties your product in a clever way, such as the "Michelle Obama arms" example.

Keep developing a list of personal PR contacts. Get to know people in the media because you're not going to send every PR in a mass mailing. You need to personally e-mail your PR contacts with the right stories.

Where, Oh Where

Fiverr.com is a site where you can basically get people to do just about anything for $5. For $5, you can hire someone to submit your PR to all the free PR sites out there. It's a good strategy, but keep in mind that most of the free PR sites don't get the syndication of the paid ones.

WebWire.com offers a $20 PR option, but once you have money to spend, PRweb is still the best, and they get excellent results but at a cost of $200. Plus, PRweb actually has a lot of information on how to write a good PR (see Figure 17.12).

Always piggyback off the news, piggyback off what's current, and piggyback off brand names. Then customize your offer. This is a great time to customize your lead magnets. This tactic alone could easily generate over 1,000 subscribers in a niche market.

Recommended PR Services

GOOD: Fiverr.com—$5 to submit to all free
press release sites

BETTER: WebWire.com—$20 press
release

BEST: PRWeb.com—$200 premium press
release service

Figure 17.12   Top three sites to use for issuing press releases.

Step 5: Viral PDFs/Infographics

Viral PDFs can easily gather your first 1,000 subscribers. Seth Godin wrote a book called *Unleashing the Idea Virus* (see Figure 17.13). Seth originally gave it away for free as a PDF, then upsold the physical book. It was an amazing success, and it publicized his brand name. You can still get a free copy as a PDF file.

Figure 17.13   You can get a free PDF version of Seth Godin's book.

PDF files are the perfect viral medium because they have a high perceived value, unlike articles, but PDF files are still easy to share. As lead magnets, PDF files prove appealing since people can print them out, interact with them, take notes on them, and save them.

The content needs to be remarkable, or it won't go viral. If something is not good or valuable, nobody's going to pass it along to their friends. You can even leverage the lead magnets that you already have. Don't hold them back as a way to get people to opt in to get it. You should have multiple lead magnets and multiple offers anyway.

The perfect viral PDF is your best stuff. Include a statement on the first page that encourages people to pass it along. That way, everybody who does opt in to your website and your inbox magazine becomes another carrier of your idea virus. Encourage it with a call to action and a link that tells readers where to get more information so they also get on your list.

To distribute PDF files, upload them to PDF distribution sites like Scribd.com, and give out your PDF files as gifts on your website and Facebook page.

If you see an inbox magazine that doesn't have a lead magnet, contact the publisher and say, "I bet you'd get more subscribers to your inbox magazine or your blog if you gave away a free report. Why don't you just give away mine?"

Another technique is to actually have a squeeze page inside your PDF. Instead of just telling people to go to an opt-in form, you can add an actual opt-in form inside the PDF. As long as people are online when reading the PDF, they could enter their e-mail address. Still keep a link in there in case the opt-in form doesn't work or if they printed out the PDF.

The secret with viral PDFs is to get them everywhere. Tell everybody you know, give it away as a gift, include it as a bonus, include it as an upsell, and put it on your thank you pages. As long as the content is good, it's going to be like a snowball rolling downhill as it goes viral. You just have to push that ball down the hill at first, then let nature do the rest.

Step 6: Ad and Resource Swaps

Resource swaps seem obvious and elementary, yet many people do not use this simple and effective strategy.

In your inbox magazine, at the end of your main essay or in the middle of your essay, display an ad. Once you've got your inbox magazine going, you can swap ads or even trade services for ads in synergistic inbox magazines. It doesn't have to be exact. What it has to be is valuable for both parties.

Don't worry if your lists aren't the same size. If you want to trade ads with somebody who has a 50,000-person list and you have a 25,000-person list, then publish that other person's ad in your inbox magazine twice.

Clearly, if you have only 1,000 people on your list, you probably can't swap ads with somebody who has a 50,000-person list. You can't say, "I'll run your ad 50 times if you run my ad once."

Rather than run ads multiple times, you can certainly offer services. For example, if you have a PR specialist supply their services to you, you can list that person on your website in exchange.

That PR specialist can have a link on your site that goes to a squeeze page. So not only are people going to use her service, they're subscribing to her inbox magazine. So it's a win-win. The number one rule with any kind of swap is that you give more than you get, especially when you are starting out.

Less Is More

When you are starting out, you need lead generation, so make sure that the service you provide for someone else for that lead generation is worth more than what you are getting. If you are doing product sales, there can be a 50/50 split if you have an even subscriber base. If not, do a 75/25 or even a 100/0 split. It doesn't matter as long as both parties walk away feeling like this is a great deal, and that you're never doing this so that you are working with somebody just once.

That's my biggest rule. If I work with somebody once on anything, chances are it wasn't a good deal for that other person. They didn't feel like they got the value they deserved. So if you want to continue the relationship, always give more than you get. This will come back to you tenfold.

If you want a double-whammy strategy guaranteed to get you subscribers, go out to affiliates and your panelists and ask them to syndicate your content. Not only give them free content, but link to your products and give them 100 percent of the affiliate commission. Now do you think they're going to want to syndicate your content? You bet they will. Do you think that if all goes well that they might mail their entire list for your offer? They would be crazy not to. It's like mailing their own product but they didn't have to do any of the work.

Are you seeing how this works? Pretty easy and straightforward.

Now you might wonder if you give someone 100 percent of the sales commission, how can you make money? You're not. At least for today. Right now, you're interested in just building your list. But it's still a win for you because you get all the names. So next time you mail your own product to your list, you keep 100 percent of the money.

Now you may be wondering how you can swap if you do not have a product to offer. That's a good question, and I have a great answer for you. When I started Working Moms Only, I did not have any product. I wrote an e-mail to folks I knew in the industry and I was fairly self-deprecating. I asked them to mail my lead magnet and said that I did not have a list to reciprocate. However, I told them that when I did, I would pay them back with 25 percent more names. So if someone mailed my lead magnet to their list of 100,000, I would mail 125,000 names to theirs once I built my own list. Others preferred me to speak at the conference while others just wanted to interview me for their subscribers.

Meanwhile, 90 percent of the folks I asked to mail did so. I had over 5,000 subscribers in 24 hours for Working Moms Only by doing only swaps. And I paid back each one of them with more than I promised.

This method also builds your reputation as someone others want to work with because you're a good person who follows through.

Low-Hanging Fruit Is Always the Way to Go

If you act on all six of these list-building strategies, you should have much more than 1,000 names. Each one of these individual strategies has yielded me thousands of names.

But you must remember that there is a real difference between doing something and doing something correctly. So when you go out there, go out with the intention to execute these strategies properly.

Make a plan, start with either the strategy that you have the most experience in or your low-hanging fruit. This way you will see results faster that will only fuel you for quicker roll-outs. And trust me, once you see the names rolling in, you will not want to stop.

PART

FINALLY, A REAL BUSINESS
OF YOUR OWN

Entrepreneurs are simply those who understand that there is little difference between obstacle and opportunity and are able to turn both to their advantage.

—Niccolo Machiavelli

18

Let's Start Monetizing: The Smart Way

Let's talk about making money to monetize your inbox magazine. First, you need to know what a reasonable monetary goal is. Your goal is to achieve between 50 cents and $1 per subscriber every month. So if you have a list size of 10,000 subscribers, your goal is to make $5,000 to $10,000 per month. Now you understand the importance of building your list from the previous chapter.

To achieve this revenue goal, you can do affiliate promotions, sell advertising, and of course, sell your own products. Indirectly, you can also monetize your list through live events and webinars, public speaking, high-dollar consulting, and book sales. Your indirect methods will most likely come after you have a sizeable list and widely recognized inbox magazine, so focus on the direct methods first.

Affiliate Promotions

The easiest way to make money with an inbox magazine is with affiliate promotions. When you are first getting started, you need to run ads. Instead of selling traditional advertisement "space," you'll be displaying ads that you wrote or revised yourself, which link to an affiliate's site.

When one of your subscribers clicks on your link and buys a product from the affiliate's site, you get a commission from that sale.

The reason affiliate programs work so well is because you're not relying on a computer to match up ads to your content. You do it yourself. You know best what ads would work with your content and which products your customers would be most interested in. When your readers see that you've taken the time to review and recommend a product, they're going to feel more comfortable buying that product.

As an inbox magazine publisher, you can get a much larger commission than what the average affiliate will make, often 50 to 100 percent higher than what may be standard in your industry by following some simple principles listed in Figure 18.1.

Nobody Likes Greedy

First, focus on building partnerships, not one-shot deals. Don't be greedy; give more than you get. It doesn't have to be about money. You might give someone a valuable service, but by the end of the day, they need to feel like they got the better deal.

When I was at Early to Rise, an advertiser didn't get the response they were expecting. They knew their ad wasn't great, but I told them I was going to show their ad to Michael Masterson and he and I were going to work on it and let them run it again. The advertiser was so happy that he later paid many times to advertise in Early to Rise.

I didn't have to help improve the ad because the advertiser knew he didn't write a very good ad and it was his fault, but I was committed to his success. That was an affiliate deal.

On an affiliate deal, you can tell your subscribers, "I used this product and it worked great for me." Offer only products that are

---

**Principles of Successful
Affiliate Deals:**

1. Build partnerships, not one-shot deals.
2. Don't be greedy; give more than you get.
3. Create win-win.
4. Offer products that are good for both partners' customers.
5. Fill a need or solve a problem.
6. Consider your long-term goals.
7. Make your partner lots of money.

Figure 18.1   How to have a successful affiliate relationship.

good for your customers. Every time you run an ad, think about products that are synergistic for you and your affiliates. Fill a need or solve a problem with those products.

Give Them What They Want

Make sure you listen to your list so you know what they say and want. At one time, subscribers to Working Moms Only wanted to learn more about using Facebook. As you know, there are hundreds of programs that claim to teach you how to make money on Facebook. So we sought out the promotion and product related to Facebook that actually taught our subscribers, over delivered on all the promises, and was priced fairly.

Many advertisers sell multiple products, so make sure you advertise the product that best matches your subscribers. The fact that they have something to sell doesn't mean you should advertise that product. See what else they have that will work to your market.

When you do well, your partners do well. Make all your partners lots of money, and you'll develop and keep long-term relationships going.

Affiliate promotions are two-way streets. Others promote for you and you promote for others. So your list should contain at least 10,000 names because when you promote for others, you want to get statistically valid data for them and for yourself.

There are plenty of inbox magazines with lists of 5,000 names doing a booming business, but when you hit 10,000 subscribers, you're in a much better position to send out affiliate promotions.

That's where you can say to others, "I'm going to mail this for you, but if I promote your offer, instead of asking for an accelerated higher affiliate commission, I want you to promote my inbox magazine and get some of your people over on my list." When you got 10,000 people, that's when you can really start making different kind of deals.

The Proof Is in the Pudding

Even after you have examined the product, you still have more due diligence before promoting any affiliate precuts. You need social proof and good metrics. First, ask about the response rate. Find out the average earnings per click (EPC). To calculate your EPC, divide your gross revenue by the numbers of clicks.

For example, if a promotion produced $50,000 in gross revenue and generated 7,000 clicks, you would divide $50,000 by 7,000. Your EPC would be $7.14. The reason this metric works is that it puts everyone on an equal playing field regardless of their list size. A baseline EPC for an information product should be at least $2, so the example of $7.14 is very good.

Next, you want to know what is being said about that particular product on social networking sites like Facebook and Twitter. Finally, ask about refund rates and any user problems with the product. Once you have done your homework, you're ready to make your deal.

When making affiliate deals, you promote others and other people promote you. If you each agreed to a 25 percent deal, you'll get 25 percent of each other's commissions. If both of your lists are approximately the same size, you'll both make the same kind of money.

You can do any kind of reciprocal deals such as saying, "I'll mail an offer to my list for you, and then you mail my offer to your list. That way, there's no affiliate tracking, and we'll each get to keep whatever money we make."

The drawback is that you could send out somebody else's offer to your list and they do great, but when that other person mails your offer to his or her list, it does terrible. Either their list is terrible or it's not the same size or quality as your own. When you do reciprocal swaps, I recommend a token amount of commission for yourself, even if it's a 10 percent affiliate, but 25 percent is better. This keeps everyone honest because they know that you're tracking their results and you know that they are tracking you.

Reciprocation is a two-way street. You mail for me and I mail for you, but it can also be, "I mail for you and I know my list has quality subscribers so you'll get a ton of responses. So if you mail for me, I expect an equal response from your subscriber list in return, especially if you are mailing proven copy."

When you start talking about 30 and 40 percent deals, you're talking about higher-end products such as high-priced coaching programs. Someone might want to sell $1,000 coaching programs with a lot of expenses involved, so they may be willing to pay you only 30 percent commission, which is fine.

A 50 percent commission is typical, but you can even go as far as taking 100 percent. That's when someone doesn't have anything to offer you. Since they can't reciprocate in any way, you can take 100 percent of that money, or vice versa.

This can also work when selling low-ticket products, like a $7, $17, or even a $47 product. That's when you say, "If I'm going to promote your offer, you need to pay me 100 percent because I know you're just doing this to build your list and plan to make money upselling them on the back end."

It's perfectly fine to get paid 100 percent, especially if you're not going to ask them to reciprocate in a similar manner. At the end of the day it all comes down to EPC. When your inbox magazine link sends a subscriber to somebody else's website, how much money is that click going to put in your pocket?

As an affiliate, you want to make sure you make at least $1 per click. If I mail for somebody selling a low-ticket offer, I have no problem telling him I need to make $1 EPC. There's no way I'm going to do it selling a product at $47, so he needs to give me 100 percent commission.

In some cases, you can even ask for more such as 125 percent or a bounty on every sale. So if someone's selling a product for $47 dollars, you can ask for $100 dollars for every sale.

The key is knowing your metrics. If you know what you should be making for every click, then you can adjust the commission to get the EPC you want. The product seller would agree if they can upsell the buyers to a higher-priced product so they're basically paying more than 100 percent commission just to add quality names to their own list.

Remember, as the inbox magazine publisher, you need to build a list of qualified people. Then you can ask for more than what advertisers would normally pay, especially if you're not asking to reciprocate.

Selling Advertising

If you sell your own products, you may think you don't need to sell any advertising. However, your subscribers will get tired of seeing your products advertised all the time. Plus, you can sell other people's advertising as a testing base.

Suppose you're thinking of developing a certain product. Before you spend the time and money to do so, advertise someone else's product to see if it's something your subscribers would buy.

That's why selling advertising in your inbox magazine can be like getting free money. Think of a typical print magazine that's all advertising driven because they don't make money from their subscription base. With an inbox magazine, this is even easier because everything is digital. Basically, there are three main advertising vehicles.

First, there are sponsored advertisings, which can be text ads, images, banners, or videos. Second, there are dedicated e-mail ads. Third, there are the website ads.

Love Those Sponsors

Sponsored ads are typically paid ads in your inbox magazine. You may ask, "How many sponsored ads can I put in there?" You can have one, two, or three ads, or banners along the side. Just make sure you're still providing quality content at all times. Then you need to test the number of ads you place in your inbox magazine to make the optimal amount of money.

If you have three ads, two can be paid and one can be yours. Or two can be yours and one can be paid. The exact number doesn't have to be the same in every issue. If people want to buy more ad space, just hold your ads back for a couple issues and test to see if your sponsor's ad is working.

In the example shown in Figure 18.2, you see a sponsored ad in the middle of the essay. As the inbox magazine publisher, you can make the ad blend in or put boxes around them to make them stand out. In this example, I placed the box around the ad and wrote the words *Sponsored Ad* for your benefit. Obviously, if you don't put boxes around the ads and don't label it as an ad, your advertisers will have better results and you can charge more, because it may be perceived as editorial content.

As a publisher, you must be committed to the success of your advertisers. You want them to do well to keep them coming back. You can't lose your integrity; you want your advertisers to succeed.

Eventually, you need to know your dollar per issue, which means you know how many dollars your inbox magazine brings in from your advertisements and which areas to place your ads so they prove to be the most lucrative. An ad appearing at the top usually performs better than a middle spot, and a middle spot will perform better than a bottom spot, so you can charge a premium for a top ad placement (see Figure 18.3).

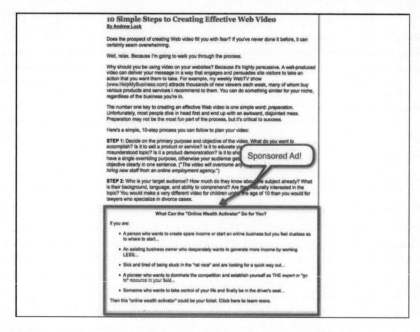

Figure 18.2   A sponsored ad can appear in the middle of your inbox magazine articles.

Figure 18.3   Ads can appear anywhere on the page.

You can even display video ads, but the videos don't actually play inside the inbox magazine. It's just a link to a video on a website. Once you've got your website set up with regular visitors, you can start selling ads on your website as well. Whether you put ads at the top, middle, bottom, or along the side of your inbox magazine, the right way is what works best for your niche.

Here are some rules of thumb about sponsored ads. The word count for a text ad should be between 10 and 100 words. I've tested this with different text ads, and 10 to 100 words works best.

If your text ad includes an image, you should have two sentences at the most. That means 10 to 20 words under or wrapped around the image for that ad. If you want to display a video ad, make that ad 30 seconds to 90 seconds long. Remember, subscribers need to get through your inbox magazine in under 10 minutes, so don't put a 10-minute video there.

You should charge an advertiser $5 to $25 per thousand for a sponsored ad in your inbox magazine. The exact number will depend on a few factors, including your niche, how many ads you place in each issue, and your open rates, which defines how many people actually read your inbox magazine issue.

So even if you have a small list of 10,000 and you have just two ads in each issue, those sponsored ads can be earning you $500 per issue. If you have four issues a month, one issue a week, your sponsored ads could make you $2,000 a month. And we haven't even talked about the more expensive advertising yet—dedicated e-mails.

Dedicated to Making Money

Dedicated e-mail ads are sent as a stand-alone promotion to a list of your qualified customers. The beauty is that there's no competition. As we just spoke about, text ads appear surrounded by articles that can distract the reader. Dedicated e-mail ads go straight to your list without having to compete for attention. Because of that, e-mail ads will be more expensive than a banner or a text ad.

A dedicated e-mail can cost $75 to $250 per thousand. That means if your list consists of 10,000 people and you charge an advertiser $100 per thousand, that advertiser may pay you $1,000 to send out their message just to a list of 10,000 subscribers.

If you send out just one inbox issue a week, you can make $4,000 a month with sponsored ads. If you send out two dedicated ads a week or eight a month, that yields $1,000 each week or $8,000 a month. Now add in your $2,000 a month from sponsored ads and your total is up to up to $10,000 a month or $120,000 a year.

At this point you should see why your goal for monetizing your inbox magazine should focus on between 50 cents and $1 per subscriber per month.

Charging $100 per thousand is actually on the low end; $200 is not out of the question. Imagine each time you send out an e-mail ad, you make $1,000 or $2,000.

The rule of thumb that works best is that for every issue you send, you can send two promotional messages. If your issue goes out once a week, sending two dedicated ads a week is fine. If your inbox magazine goes out twice a week, you can send up to four promotional messages a week.

You Can Be Direct or Indirect

When you send out dedicated e-mail ads, you can choose a direct or indirect endorsement. With a direct endorsement, you make sure everyone knows you're endorsing that particular ad and giving it your seal of approval. In the example in Figure 18.4, notice that the ad has my Working Moms Only header just like subscribers would see on my inbox magazine issues.

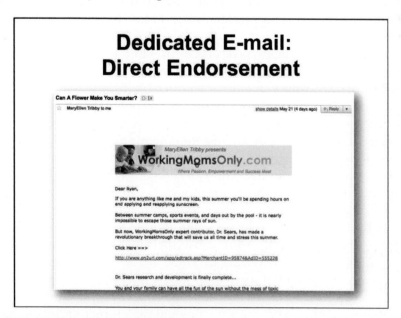

Figure 18.4   A direct endorsement ad example.

Because Dr. Sears is on my panel, I remind them that he is an expert on the WorkingMomsOnly.com panel. If you scroll down the ad, you would see that it's signed "Cheers, ME," just like I sign every issue.

You don't want to have it signed generically like "Sincerely, the Working Moms Only advertising team." That would make people think, "Maybe MaryEllen hasn't looked at this and doesn't really trust it." Direct endorsements will make you more money than an implied endorsement.

An implied endorsement is still a dedicated e-mail; however, it does not contain the same personalized elements of a direct endorsement. It will usually not personalize the reader's first name. Instead, it may say "Dear Reader." The message is usually brief and may say, "Please see the message from our advertiser." And then the company, not a person such as the publisher or editor, likely signs it.

You are doing your advertisers a disservice when you send out ads as an implied endorsement. It's pretty much the same thing as saying, "Hey, I did not review or even look at this product. But since this company sent me money to send this message to you, I did."

You should always keep your list in the forefront to protect and advocate for your subscribers. That's why even though you would get paid to advertise certain product, you will need to say "no" to some of them.

Just as with affiliate products, you want to make sure paid-advertisement products are good for your community. You don't need to preface your e-mail with a notice like: "This is an advertisement" or "This is sponsored mail." Some people do this because they're not always advocating for their subscribers or vetting the product. That means they are just looking for a check.

As long as you always keep your subscribers number one, you'll make more money because you can sell your advertising for more. Your advertisers can make more money because you aren't cutting their legs out from under them and saying, "I don't know anything about this guy, but he gave me some money so you might want to listen to what he said." Your subscribers benefit because you're advocating for them by vetting products before offering it to them. The direct endorsement model absolutely works better.

Indirect endorsements just tell you that they got paid to send out the ad. If they were to send this out as a direct endorsement, the message could come across more personal, such as, "Hey, Bob here, publisher of XYZ Company. I just wanted to say I ran across something that may interest you and I think you should take a look. Here it is." That would obviously perform better.

Don't think it always has to be one or the other—direct or implied. You just need to understand the distinction between direct and implied endorsement so you can decide what you want to do and when.

However, you need to approve everything that comes from your advertisers. Here are some rules of thumb for dedicated e-mails. Earlier, I told you that the word count for text ads should be between 10 and 100 words. For dedicated e-mail ads, the word count needs to be between 100 and 400 words. You want people to get into the ad. It's dedicated, so you have that space to do so.

You can sell partial or full drops. A partial drop is selling to part of your list, and a full drop is selling to your entire list. Once your list gets large enough, you can do both. You'll need at least 40,000 subscribers before you can start doing partial drops. Until then, you'll need to do full drops to your entire subscriber list.

Again, think about two advertisements for every content piece in your inbox magazine. If you promote too many dedicated e-mails, people will start losing interest in your content because they're getting inundated with too many ads.

For folks just getting started, start with sending one issue per week, then two as you start to grow. Keep in mind that two-to-one ratio so there are never more than two advertisements for every content piece.

Now, what do you need to get started? You need a rate card, also known as a data card. You will eventually need a media kit, and you're going to need some list brokers and some list managers. So let's discuss that now.

Rates and Data: It's All in the Cards

Now that you understand the different kind of ads you can sell, let's talk about how you do that, how much you charge, and how advertisers can keep you on their radar screen.

Let's start with a rate or data card to start selling advertising in your inbox magazine (see Figure 18.5). A rate or data card contains standardized information on how you developed your list, along with pertinent information such as pricing, demographic, and psychographic details.

To create a data card you should have at least 5,000 names. That's a must because most advertisers can't make enough money with any list smaller than 5,000 names.

A typical data card consists of the following:

1. List name
2. List universal pricing
3. List description
4. Demographic information
5. Advertising specifications
6. List updates
7. Gender breakouts
8. Minimum order
9. Source
10. Media
11. Unit of sale
12. Net name policy
13. Usage

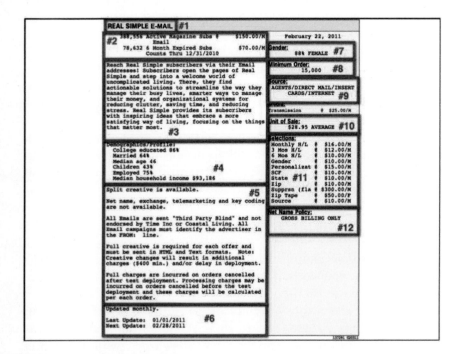

Figure 18.5   Sample rate or data card.

Number 1 displays the name of the list, which in this case is "Real Simple." *Real Simple* is actually the name of a print magazine with an online presence. This data card is for the e-mail names that subscribe to the *Real Simple* e-letter.

Number 2 is the list size, also known as the universe. You can see the pricing where they're charging $150 per thousand. That "/M" means per thousand, not million because the M is a Roman numeral that stands for 1,000. This rate card says they have 388,000 active e-mail subscribers and also 78,000 expired subscribers who didn't renew their subscription. That's why the expired subscription list is less expensive.

You don't have to rent all 388,000 names. If you look at number 8, you can order a minimum of 15,000. Multiply 15 by $150 to equal $2,250. That means they won't rent their list for less than $2,250, which is their minimum order.

If you rent the entire list, you're talking 388 times $150 or a cost of $58,200. If you owned the *Real Simple* e-mail list, you could make $58,200 every time somebody wanted to send an e-mail to your inbox magazine subscribers. Typically, people don't pay the full rate card amount, so you'll actually earn less.

If someone rents your list multiple times, you can give them a discount. At Early to Rise, we had 200,000 subscribers, and I quickly built that list to 450,000 subscribers. That added incremental revenue because people were already renting that list. All of a sudden, the revenue from list rental more than doubled.

If you are renting somebody else's list, start out with their active subscribers. If that works for you, test their expired subscribers. Don't start off renting the entire list. Start out with a much smaller number and then scale up. Tell that to your advertisers, too. You want them to be successful, so tell them to take a segment of your list and come back once it they have tested it.

Number 3 simply describes the list. Who are these people? When reading the description, keep in mind that it's sales copy. They're calling out to the type of advertisers they want, such as advertisements to help people manage their busy lives, smarter ways to manage money, or systems for reducing clutter and saving time. They're saying, "Hey, if you're selling something on organization, money management, reducing stress, or saving time and money, then this is for you." So you want to describe your subscribers and reach out to the types of advertisers you would want as well.

Number 4 is the demographic profile: whether the subscribers are college educated, married, the median age, number of children, employment, and their median household income.

Number 5 defines the advertising specifications. The most important part to notice on this card is where it says, "All Emails are sent Third party Blind and not endorsed by Time Inc. . . ." What this means is even though this list is made up of Real Simple subscribers and owned by Time Inc., the "from" line will be from the renter. You do not want to do this on your data card. As a matter of fact, you should put that "E-mails are not blind," or you might say direct endorsements available and how much extra they may cost. (We will talk about premium pricing, known as selects, in a moment.)

Number 6 tells you how often the rate card information gets updated. If it's updated monthly, new names will appear and other names may drop off.

Number 7 talks about gender. A rate card might say 88 percent female or 12 percent male. This one just says it's mostly female.

Number 8 specifies the minimum order, which is 15,000. If your list is under 25,000 names, you should require a full rental agreement.

Number 9 lists the source that explains where the names came from, such as agents, direct mail, insert cards, and the Internet. That means subscribers are finding Real Simple through direct mail agents, direct mail, insert cards, and online advertising. For most inbox magazines, your main source will largely be the Internet.

Number 10 is the unit of sale, which is also known as the average unit of sale (AUS). Here, the AUS is $28.95. If an advertiser wants to sell a $5,000 coaching program, it may not work with your audience because the AUS is only $28.95. If your AUS is $1,000 and somebody wants to sell a $900 home study kit, that's a better fit.

If your inbox magazine is not currently selling any of your own products, then you would just leave this unit of sale section off completely. The AUS applies only if you have your own product that you are selling to your subscribers.

Number 11 offers different selects. Any time you order an additional select, you will be charged a premium per thousand. When you look at this data card you will see 3 Mos H/L and 6 Mos H/L. That stands for three-month hotlines and six-month hotlines.

Hotlines are your most recent additions to the list. Since recent subscribers usually increase the response rate, there is a premium charge. If advertisers want to target the subscribers you received in the past month, they'll have to pay an extra $16 per thousand. If they just want people who subscribed in the past three months, it will cost them $12 dollars. Six months, $10. If you're adding a lot of new subscribers every month, just selling those hotline subscribers is a great way to make additional revenue. You can even select subscribers based on gender, state, zip code, or source.

In the beginning, when your inbox magazine has only 5,000, 10,000, or 20,000 subscribers, you won't need to offer all the selections we discussed. Just start with a very simple data card that would include list name, list size, the description of your list, and your advertising specifications. This will serve you well to start.

Evolution in Advertising

Just like everything, your website, your inbox magazine, and your data card will evolve. And new promotional material will be required. One of those promotional materials is a media kit.

A media kit is essentially just an advertisement for your advertisers. Even though you do not need one at first, eventually you will need one because you want to make it as easy as possible for companies to advertise with you. Your media kit is the document that you invite companies to view when they want to advertise in your inbox magazine or on your website. It should reflect your inbox magazine brand. Use the same color scheme, graphics, and style that emphasize your brand. Keep it consistent because consistency matters. You do not want to confuse your advertiser or they will shy away.

Next, you need an elevator pitch that basically explains what you do. A lot of people think an elevator pitch is 30 seconds, but an elevator pitch is actually 17 seconds, which is the average time it takes an elevator to go from one floor to the next, so be ready to explain what you do in 17 seconds or less.

You need an explanation of your niche. After you have stated your elevator pitch, explain your inbox magazine niche, and why you are an important part of that niche. Most important, how are advertisers going to benefit?

List any traffic statistics from your inbox magazine and your website. Be completely honest. People can visit sites like Compete .com, Quantcast, and Alexa to double check your numbers. If you lie to them, they'll find out and never do business with you. Don't set false expectations. Be realistic about your subscriber counts and your traffic numbers and charge accordingly. Always shoot for a long-term relationship.

Your media kit also needs to include your advertising options and guidelines. This is where you explain the cost per issue, per week, and per month. Explain any discounts you might offer for advertisers who book three issues versus one, or six issues versus one.

Include the sizes and all specifications for any kind of banners. You might say you cannot have more than 50 or 100 words in your texts ad, or that images can't be above a certain size. Be clear about how you'll be paid and when you must receive payment.

Let's look at the media kit for Newsmax.com shown in Figure 18.6. Newsmax doesn't just state its demographics; it actually gives you some nice graphs and charts that break it all down. It lists the different ad sizes for its print magazine such as full page, ⅔ page, ½ page, etc. They also list the frequency such as one time, three times, six times, or 12 times. The more people advertise, the lower the rate goes per each advertisement.

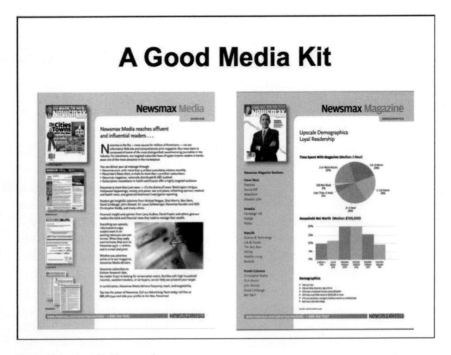

Figure 18.6   A media kit example.

If you publish weekly, a good rule of thumb for paid advertising is to be working three weeks ahead of time. Start banking your advertisements ahead of time just like you do for your content.

Remember, not only can you accept advertising inside your inbox magazine itself, you can also have sponsored ads and dedicated e-mails going out to your list.

In the old days with printed magazines, media kits were expensive to produce and mail. For an inbox magazine, your media kit just needs to appear on your website at virtually no cost to you.

With your inbox magazine, there are essentially two ways to make money: a flat fee and a cost per thousand. You will probably charge a flat fee until you have a list of 40,000. Then you can start charging a cost per thousand and segmenting your list.

To determine what flat fee you can charge, ask yourself what your market warrants. Look at the rate cards for other inbox magazines in your niche, and then start just below your competition. Let the advertisers be successful, and then take your rates up eventually.

If advertisers keep coming back, that's a great sign because that means they're getting their return on investment (ROI). If they spent $1,000 and they've made more than $1,000, they are going to come back. Ask your advertisers how well they did. If they got a 300 percent ROI, chances are you'll be able to raise your rates in the upcoming year.

Look to your competitors for your price, and know your key metrics. Understand your open rates and click-through rates and how much you make per issue. If you understand how much you make per issue with an affiliate mailing or with your own product, that's going to give you a place to start for your flat-fee pricing.

Brokers and Managers

Now let's answer the question about list brokers versus list managers.

A list broker finds you lists to send your promotions to and looks for places to advertise your inbox magazine. A list manager manages and rents your list to other advertisers. You want a list manager to manage your list. However, don't contact a list manager until you have at least 5,000 people on your list.

List managers get paid on a commission basis. When they rent your list, they typically receive 15 to 20 percent and you get the rest of the money. They are going to do all the work for you, even collect the money and send you a check.

The list manager spends their own money advertising in industry trade journals, associations, and conferences. In collaboration with you, they will even put together your rate card.

Once a list manager has an advertiser for you, they send you the advertiser's copy. You need to make sure that the copy and product is a good fit for your subscribers and that you are proud to endorse it.

Once you have approved the marketing piece, you need to agree on an e-mail deployment date. Now here is the very important part. Never turn your list over to anyone. You are the one sending your advertiser's message to your list.

Remember, advertisers do not buy your list, they rent your list. If you give them your list, you will be considered a "spammer," and your business will be in jeopardy of being shut down.

Logical and Methodical

As you can see, there are multiple ways to make money from your inbox magazine, but don't feel you have to do all of them at once. But they are all very logical and methodical, so start with one method and as you see results and gain confidence, branch out and try the other methods. It doesn't matter which method you start with just as long as you get started.

When you're creating your inbox magazine, focus on delivering the best content possible. Then worry about the best ads for your target audience. When you put your subscribers' interests first, the advertising will take care of itself and you should start to see the money.

Remember to look to your competition to see what they are doing and how they are dealing with advertising. Your job will be to do it better and faster.

CHAPTER 19

The Publisher's Matrix: Your Content Empire

Now that you know how to make money promoting affiliate products and selling advertising, you need to learn about the publisher model and how to create your own products, like printed books, e-books, subscription sites, and multimedia home study courses (see Figures 19.1 through 19.4).

Creating content and teaching can be fun, but what's even better is when someone else creates it but you get to publish it and collect the money. Think about the difference between a professional athlete and the owner of the team. I would love to own a team (preferably the Yankees) and watch all the players each game, knowing that I can afford to pay them because I'm making the money to do so.

Or think about Oprah starting out with just one show—her own. With just one show, she was responsible for all the content that she delivered each episode. Now that she owns an entire network with multiple shows, she doesn't need to create the content for every show. She simply gives it a thumbs up or down. That's what the inbox publisher can be like, and that's the mind-set you need to adopt.

As an inbox magazine publisher, you can make money through advertising revenue and affiliate revenue. Start thinking like a publisher, not just how to be a guru or an author.

For example, I published a product that was called "The Ultimate Working Moms Only Mindset: Seven Easy Steps to Achieving a Prosperous, Purposeful and Happy Life." This was a multimedia website for members only, but I didn't create all the content. That's

The Ultimate Working Moms Only Mindset

Seven Easy Steps to Achieving a Prosperous, Purposeful and Happy Life

ACTIVITY JOURNAL

By PJ McClure

Figure 19.1   Publish printed books.

because I created this product and others using the four publishing content methods we are about to go over.

In all these cases, you do not have to be the one creating the product. However, you can be the one depositing the checks. Four ways to create a product are:

1. Partner with experts.
2. Buy or license existing content.
3. Hire ghostwriters to create content.
4. Interview experts.

Figure 19.2   Publish e-books.

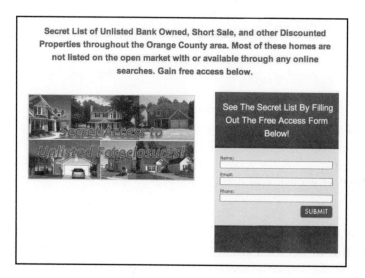

Figure 19.3   Publish subscription sites.

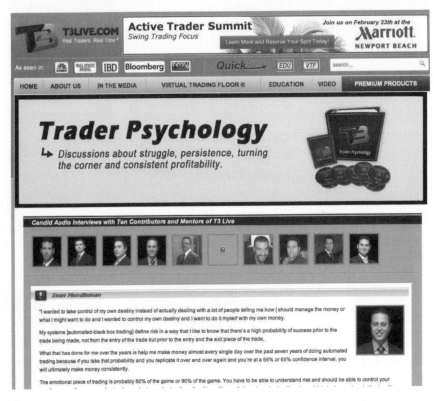

Figure 19.4   Publish multimedia courses.

A joint venture partnership with an expert means the expert creates the product, you market it to your list, and you split the profits, such as 50/50, or 75/25.

If the content already exists, you can buy it outright for a flat fee and then all future profits go directly to you, or you can license the content, which means splitting the profits with the content author. If you hire a ghostwriter, you can keep most or all of the profits and just pay the ghostwriter a flat fee or a percentage of the royalties.

If you interview an expert, you can sell the audio recordings or get the audio transcribed and edited to sell as a printed book. Which method you use depends on the type of content (see Figure 19.5).

Publisher Model Matrix

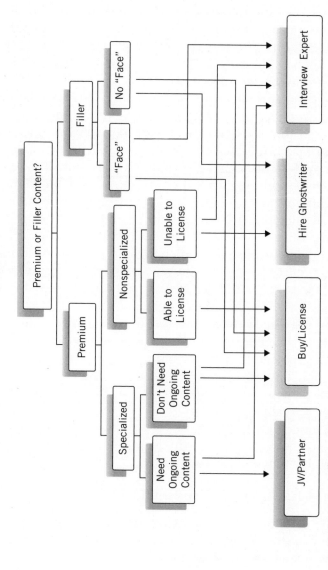

Figure 19.5   Deciding how to publish content.

Determine Your Needs

First, ask if this is premium content or filler content. Premium content represents a major product, not just an article or a bonus that you attach to another product. That's filler content.

Next, is it specialized or nonspecialized? Products geared toward the financial trading market are more specialized than similar products geared for the fitness market. That's because there are a lot of fitness trainers who know the same information, but there are far fewer financial trading experts.

If the content is filler, you don't need a face or story behind it, so that's a great opportunity to hire a ghostwriter or buy or license content. You can also interview experts to create additional filler content.

If you do need a face on the product, then buy or license the content. With "The Ultimate Working Moms Only Mindset: Seven Easy Steps to Achieving a Prosperous, Purposeful and Happy Life," P. J. McClure is the face of this product. He's the true expert with a fantastic reputation, so it would have been foolish to strip his brand from the product.

When you partner with somebody, you typically need to pay an ongoing royalty every time you make a sale. If it's nonspecialized content, then you should license it. If you can't license the content, hire a ghostwriter or interview an expert.

If you just need to sell a product that you won't need to update often, then buy or license. If it is premium, specialized content, then do a joint venture partnership.

The only time you should enter into a long-term joint venture, partnership, or royalty agreement with an expert is when you need premium, specialized content that needs regular updating. For any other instance, buy it, license it, hire a ghostwriter, or interview an expert. That way, you pay nothing, pay very little, or just make a one-time payment and be done with it.

Publisher Method 1: Joint Venture Partnerships

There are two options with joint venture partnerships: partner with a known expert or develop an unknown expert. Both options have their advantages and disadvantages.

Partnering with a known expert is faster and easier because she already has credibility. Maybe she's written a book or published some articles, so she has a proven ability to create content.

The cons are that you have less control and will typically get a smaller share of the profits. Known experts are usually better businesspeople, so they can be harder to deal with and have larger egos. When you come across people with a huge ego, pass on them. There are enough experts out there who are good people, so you shouldn't ever put up with someone who is arrogant.

When it comes to developing unknown experts, they are typically easier to negotiate with, so you have greater control of the business. In fact, you could take 100 percent of the company and just pay them a small royalty. Unknown experts tend to have smaller egos and are easier to work with.

The cons can be a slower process because an unknown expert may never have created content before, and there is no guarantee that she'll be able to create content consistently.

Either way, it's not a question of working with an unknown expert or a known expert, but whoever will be the best fit for your product and your customers. As an inbox magazine publisher, you already have panelists, and your panelists will be your best source of experts to publish.

Your panelists should be people with an interesting hobby, talent, or skill who solved a major problem in their own life. They may have lost a lot of weight, helped a loved one through an illness, landed a great job, or survived a bankruptcy or divorce.

When it comes to working with experts, authors can consistently create content, and many of them just want to get their content out to the public. Plus, they might have gotten paid a small advance from a publisher to write their book, and maybe that book sold a couple thousand copies and earned only a few thousand dollars. Now you have the chance to help authors publish their products. This is a win-win because you help them make bigger money while you get your fair share as well. To find published authors, just do a search in Amazon.

Another great source is locating authors of out-of-print books (see Figure 19.6). Visit Bookfinder.com or Alibris.com. Authors whose books are out of print aren't making much money off their books, so they may be very open to doing a deal. Also, when books go out of print, sometimes the rights to that content revert from the publisher back to the original author. That means you may be able to repurpose and republish the book as an e-book, home study course, or membership site.

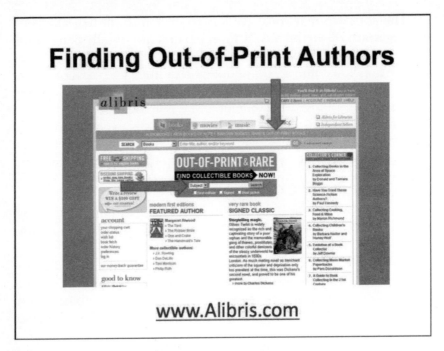

Figure 19.6   Finding out-of-print authors.

Also look for gurus who might be doing public speaking, running coaching programs, or selling products of their own. Look for gurus selling products on ClickBank.com or search Google and look for products with high search engine optimization rankings.

Also look for regular contributors to industry journals or magazines because they can write and create content. Do a Google search for your market name with the word *forum* after it, and you'll find dedicated forums.

When it's time to do the deal, ask yourself who's putting up the money and taking the risk. If you're publishing someone and he is just providing content, is isn't risking much. If things don't work out, he won't lose any money. So if you're taking the risk, that's going to affect the deal.

Another factor to consider is who will be doing the ongoing work? If you're working with an expert who will provide monthly, weekly, or daily updates, he's going to want a bigger piece of the pie. If he just hands over a product without future updates, then buy it outright or license the content.

Who is funding the start-up costs? That person deserves the lion's share of the profits. What if the business loses money? You need to talk about this up front. Finally, will there be a noncompete clause? If you are going to lock him down and prevent him from selling his products on his own or working with any other people, then you need to give him a bigger piece of the deal.

Start Simply

The first typical deal structure is a straight 50/50 partnership. In this case, both parties should invest their own cash. If you're going to have a partner, you want a partner who will share in both the profits and losses. If your company makes $10,000 in one month, then your partner should get $5,000 for that month. However, if your company loses $10,000 the next month, your partner needs to write a check to the company for the same $5,000. He should be a partner in the upside as well as the downside. That's a discussion that needs to take place with any potential partner.

The fact that you are paying him 50 percent of the money doesn't mean he necessarily gets 50 percent of the company. There are both equity and royalty deals.

J. K. Rowling, the author of the Harry Potter books, most likely doesn't have an equity stake in her publisher, but I'm sure she's got a very nice royalty deal. I would avoid giving away equity to a content creator. If somebody's not going to be a partner on the upside as well as the downside, then he's not really an equity partner.

The second type of deal structure is an 80/20 partnership. That means you get 80 percent and they get a 20 percent royalty. This is best if only one person is investing money, but both are providing intellectual capital.

If you are the one making the cash register ring and taking all the risk, then you deserve the lion's share of the money. Keep in mind that a typical book publishing deal is usually somewhere between 8 and 15 percent. If you are doing 80/20 deal, your content provider should be extremely satisfied.

Your ability to market and run the business is just as valuable, if not more, than the actual content. If you're investing $20,000 dollars in a deal, then the first $20,000 that comes in should pay you back. After you get paid back, then you start splitting the profits 80/20. Sometimes these deals can switch to 50/50 once the investing party gets paid back.

As a general rule, never pay more than 30 percent royalty. If somebody doesn't understand that, explain the royalty on a traditional book publishing deal. Then remind him that you are taking all the risk and doing the bulk of the work.

One of the best ways to work with an expert is through a flat-fee joint venture. He is not a partner or earning a royalty. Instead, he just gets a flat fee to create the product, whether a one-time payment or ongoing monthly payments. This is good if the publisher is investing all the money and the expert is unknown.

Percentage Work

The fourth type of deal structure is a percentage of earnings or a royalty. Sometimes experts don't want a flat-fee deal, but will accept a royalty of 10, 15, or 20 percent. When doing a royalty calculation, don't calculate royalties based on gross sales or revenues. Calculate royalties after your expenses such as traffic costs, affiliate commissions, taxes, merchant fees, and cost of goods sold (COGS) if it's a physical product.

Let's say you sold $10,000 dollars of a given product, but it cost you $2,000 dollars to fulfill. Take the $2,000 off and pay their 20 percent royalty out of $8,000. You have expenses for customer support, refunds, traffic costs, taxes, merchant fees, and any additional overhead. Subtract those costs from the remaining $8,000 before you pay the royalty. Never pay a royalty on gross revenues until you calculate all expenses.

Publisher Method 2: Buying and Licensing Content

Licensing or buying content is the fastest and easiest way to get content for a membership site, e-book, or for any other type of premium content. You don't have to work with an expert to create content. Just find content that you like and buy it for a one-time fee.

You can buy private label rights, which means you buy somebody else's content and then have the right to rename, modify, or rewrite it. You can also buy standard rights, which means you own the rights to sell somebody's product but you can't take their name off it or change the title since it's still their product.

To find content to buy, research your options. First, start with ClickBank, which is a site where people sell digital products such as e-books (see Figure 19.7). ClickBank displays a proprietary score or

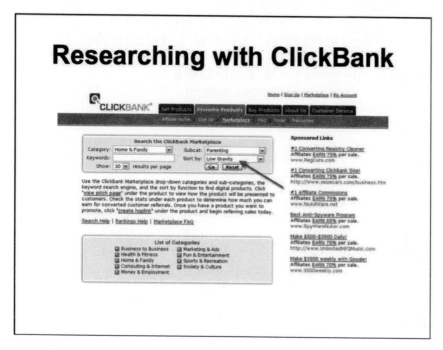

Figure 19.7   Look for ClickBank products with low gravity.

indicator known as a "gravity score," so search for products related to your market. Now look for those products that have a low gravity because those are the products that are not selling well even if they're high-quality products. You can also locate content sites using Google.

Always buy and review any product you're thinking about licensing. This is not optional. You don't want to spend money on a license only to find out that the product is inferior.

Just like buying real estate, look for products and websites that look dumpy with bad titles and ugly designs, but the content itself is good (see Figure 19.8). Real estate investors love finding a house that has ugly carpet and a really bad paint job but with a good floor plan in a great neighborhood. That's because they know they can make a lot of money on it just by doing minor repairs like painting and putting in new carpet.

That's how you have to approach these websites. When searching for home and family parenting topics, I ran across this website. As you can see, it is not very pleasing to the eye. But if the

Figure 19.8   An example of an ugly website that might be selling a great product.

content is great, I don't care if the website is ugly. For my market of Working Moms Only, some working moms are single moms and may get into custody disputes, so this might be a great product to buy or license.

Besides looking for products on ClickBank and ugly websites, contact authors whose books have gone out of print and see if they'll license the content to you.

Once you have three to five products that you might like to buy or license, it's time to make the initial offer. You may be worried that if you make offers to three to five people, what happens if they all come back and say yes?

The reason you want to make three to five offers is that most of the people you contact won't respond. So if you contact three to five people, you may hear back from at least one of them. On the off chance that you hear back from all five of them, you're not sending out contracts yet, so this is a good problem to have. You can retract your offer to some of the sites or products and do a deal later.

When you make the initial offer, say as little as possible in the initial e-mail (see Figure 19.9). Just check to see if they are remotely

First Contact Script

I was wondering if you would be open to selling a private label license to your product, [ENTER PRODUCT NAME]. I enjoyed the content very much and would I like to be able to sell a similar product.

The license would essentially let me use your content in a product of my own in exchange for a one-time payment. It would also allow you to continue selling the product however you like.

We can obviously discuss the details, but first I wanted to see if this is something you would be interested in and how much you would want for such a license.

Figure 19.9   A sample script for how to contact potential licensees.

interested. If you go into detail about the deal you want to make, the chance of their saying no or not replying is much higher than if you reach out subtly.

Tell them that you'd love to license their content and ask how much it would cost. Most people won't quote a price, so have a price in mind that you are willing to pay. If I'm willing to spend $1,000 dollars to license content, then quote them a price that's 25 to 50 percent of what you are willing to spend. That leaves room for negotiating.

Don't get too pushy or sound like a lawyer. If people feel intimidated, their response is most likely going to be no.

First, mention why you're contacting that person (to buy or license their content). Then explain that licensing the content still allows her to continue selling the content on her own. By adding that one line, your response rate will increase. Most of these individuals spent a lot of time creating their product, so even if they're not making much money from it, they don't want to give up on their dream.

The third paragraph lets them consider a license deal and that's it. The whole idea is to plant the idea how much they would like for a license. Usually they'll ask you to make an offer first, and if your offer sounds fair, you'll have a good chance of getting a deal.

Be creative and a little bit flexible. You may want to remove their name from the product, but they may insist on keeping their name on the product. They might know that they aren't making any money from sales on their own, but it is still their creation and they don't want to have themselves completely removed from it.

Also, never speak disparagingly about a product to try to get a better deal. Don't say something obtuse, mean, or rude. If you tell them that their product needs help, they are not going to want to do the deal with you no matter how badly they may need the money. Always be complimentary.

The third step is to actually do the deal. Know from the start how much you are willing to spend. Only you know how much money your business is making and how much you can afford to spend. Do you have more money or do you have more time? At the end of the day, you're licensing content to make more money off that content than it cost you. Whether you pay $2,000, $5,000, $10,000, or $20,000 doesn't matter as long as you feel confident that you'll make all your money back and earn a hefty profit as well.

Publisher Method 3: Hiring Ghostwriters

Hiring ghostwriters to create content can often be just as expensive as, or even more expensive than, buying or licensing content, and there's really no guarantee of success. You hire somebody and hope that they do a good job.

However, if you can't find anything to license, can't get any deals done, and don't have time to create it yourself, that's the time to hire a ghostwriter.

Make sure that you work with real experts, not just ghostwriters who happen to be good researchers. For example, if you need to hire somebody to write a course on stock trading, hire a ghostwriter who also actively trades stocks. If you are going to hire somebody to create a quilting manual, have her show you some of the quilts that she made herself. You don't want ghostwriters who are good researchers. You want real experts; otherwise, they'll sound fake.

I once needed some special reports written for my Working Moms Only Success Club. So we hired two ghostwriters to write the same report. One was a man, Brad. He was young and single with no children. He had excellent references, and his writing samples were very good.

The other was a woman, Karen. She was middle aged and married with two children. She, too, had excellent references, and her writing samples were very good as well.

Hands down, Karen's report was so much better. It was engaging, authentic, educational, and entertaining. Whereas Brad's was well written, it lacked the engagement and excitement that Karen's report exuded. Clearly, her years of being an expert working mom made the difference.

Go Fishing Where the Fish Are

Two sources for finding ghostwriters include eLance and Guru.com (see Figure 19.10). Just search your market and add the word *writer*. That way, instead of finding a stock trader, a yoga instructor, or a professional fisherman, you'll find a writer who is a stock trader, a yoga instructor, or a professional fisherman. After you find several possible ghostwriters, check out their reviews and feedback (see Figure 19.11).

Figure 19.10   Searching for a ghostwriter on Guru.com.

Figure 19.11   Viewing a list of possible ghostwriters.

Some other resources for ghostwriters include people who have written books or magazine articles about your topic. When hiring ghostwriters, tighten the focus of your content for better results. Don't ask for an e-book on how to play online poker because that's way too broad.

Give them a specific subject such as a training product that provides step-by-step instructions on how to build the ultimate tree house. Make sure you get those specific actionable content elements.

Time is of the essence, so never hire just one ghostwriter. Instead, hire three to five writers and pay them $50 to $100 each to write an outline and an introduction. The reason is that an outline ensures that the product covers everything that you want. Plus, the introduction gives you an idea of their writing style and their voice.

Here's an ingenious little trick. Hire the writer who has the best introduction, and give them the best outline. Sometimes the person who wrote the best introduction didn't necessarily write the best outline, but since you paid for them all, you own them and you can use them all.

Set hard deadlines and make payments only when milestones are reached. Never pay 100 percent of the money in advance. Always make them deliver before they get paid. If you pay them all up front, then they have no motivation in any way, shape, or form to do a good job or to do a quick job. Expect to pay $5 to $15 per page, so a 100-page e-book might cost between $500 and $1,500, depending on your market.

Make sure you run some snippets of their content through Copyscape.com. This verifies that the ghostwriter is delivering original content and not just copying stuff off the Internet. That's called copyright infringement. Even though they are the ones who violated it, if you go and sell somebody else's copyrighted content, you will ultimately be held liable.

Figure 19.12 is a sample project for requesting a table of contents and an outline. You want to specify that all work delivered must be original and absolutely not violate any copyright. Also make sure the ghostwriter agrees to keep the nature of this writing assignment and the content strictly confidential.

Most important, state that all deliverables will be considered work for hire in the U.S. copyright law. That means that you own all the copyright after you pay the ghostwriter.

Make sure you specify that the writing must meet a fifth-grade level (or whatever level you choose) so it will be easy to read. The standard for most books and newspapers is that all articles should be written to a fifth-grade level.

Also specify copy standards, headlines, and subheads such as 18-point Tahoma for headlines and 12-point Arial for text (see Figure 19.13). That's because if you request a 50-page report, you don't want a 50-page report that's been padded in 18 point Times New Roman font with double spacing.

Specify a word count and specify your project as clearly as possible. The more specific that you can get, the better the results you will get.

Publisher Method 4: Interviewing Experts

Interviewing experts is the easiest and cheapest way to get content. It can even be free if you interview your multitude of panelists and create a product to sell.

A great method is to interview multiple experts and create a compilation product. Not only do you get more content, but you

Table of Contents
Sample Project

I am currently seeking a writer to create an outline or a table of contents for a book that I am writing on _____. In order to do a good job you should look at outlines from other books or e-books on the subject, if any exist, on Amazon.com using the "look inside" feature.

Each letter will be created by the following process. I cannot stress how important it is that the order of the letter must be followed.

I will provide you with product details and our unique selling position.

You don't have to be an award-winning writer to create effective tables of contents. In fact, writing great tables of contents is more of a science than an art. Even the pros use proven "templates" to create tables of contents that get results.

Deliverables

1) All work delivered must be original and absolutely not violate any copyright. Service Provider must agree to indemnify Buyer and take full responsibility for any costs of any copyright infringement action including damages and attorney's fees should they occur. This should be no problem if your work is original.

2) Service provider agrees to keep the nature of his/her writing assignments and the fact that the content will be published under the name of the Buyer strictly confidential.

3) All work shall be delivered to the Buyer in individual text files as they are completed and shall be spell checked and fact-checked.

4) All deliverables will be considered "work made for hire" under U.S. copyright law. Seller will assign and Buyer will receive exclusive and complete copyrights to all work purchased. (No GPL, GNU, 3rd party components, etc. unless all copyright ramifications are explained to AND AGREED TO by the buyer of the site per the coder's Seller Legal Agreement.)

5) All work must start within (3) business days of award and must be completed at a minimum rate of (1) table of contents per (1) U.S. business days after the start date. To be clear on this point, you will be expected to have e-mailed (1) table of contents before 11:59 PM CST on the 4th U.S. business day after being awarded the job.

Figure 19.12   A sample project proposal.

Complete Project Sample Project

Report Creation Guide

Hi, I need an experienced writer to create a simple, easy to read report on [SUBJECT]. The report should be approximately 2,000 words long and rich with useful information, links to supportive images, or illustrations.

I will provide you with an outline and an audio interview on the subject, plus any other research documents that I have, but further research on your part will be required.

The report should be written from the point of an expert on [SUBJECT], and it should instruct the reader step-by-step on what to do to reach their goal of [GOAL] in the shortest amount of time possible.

Even though the information may be simple, it must be made to sound profound and top secret. Our site provides "Secret Reports" to our reader as our theme and this must be conveyed in each report.

You must write at a 4th grade level with short sentences and plenty of line breaks for skimming. Think about readability.

Headlines should be 18pt Tahoma and type should be 12pt Arial.

Bold or highlight major points.

Use lists and bullet points as often as possible.

Figure 19.13   Another sample project letter.

get the dynamic of having two or more experts offering different information.

You can also become an expert by association. The best example of all this is Napoleon Hill, who wrote *Think and Grow Rich*. Napoleon Hill was not a personal growth expert but a journalist (see Figure 19.14). He just interviewed rich, successful people and turned their thoughts into a best-selling book.

Here is how the interview process works:

1. Brainstorm a list of potential experts that you can interview.
2. Contact those experts.
3. Create a hard-to-refuse offer.
4. Develop a series of questions.
5. Conduct the interview.

If you start with your panelists, you've already done steps 1 and 2. Your ideal interviewee is someone who has created products,

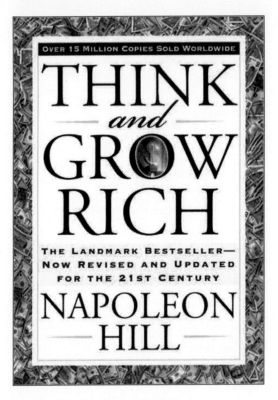

Figure 19.14   *Think and Grow Rich* is a classic self-help book.

written books, or published articles in your niche. You also want people who have accolades and awards.

One of the best sources for experts is RTIR.com. If you recall, RTIR.com is a site where experts pay to be listed so radio and TV reporters will find and invite them onto their show. If they're willing to be interviewed for some small local TV show or radio station, they'll probably be willing to do an interview with you as well.

Once you've identified your experts, contact them. Each request needs to be personalized. Don't send out mass mailing (see Figure 19.15).

Introduce yourself and explain that for your business, you interview industry experts. Explain how you found them through their book, product, or article, and ask if they'd be interested in doing an interview about a specific topic. That's it, very simple.

Initial Contact Script

Hi _____,

My name is _____ and I own and operate YourSite.com, a
subscription site in the _____ industry. Every month I do an
interview with an industry expert for my subscribers, and after reading
your book/product/article/etc., _____, it's clear
that you fall into that category.

Would you be open to doing an interview about [insert topic idea] (or
whatever else you'd like to discuss) in the coming weeks?

I look forward to your reply,
[YOUR NAME]

Figure 19.15   Creating a contact script.

Once you've made that initial contact, entice them with a hard-to-refuse offer. Most people are happy just to do an interview for free just for the exposure to plug their book or product. If they balk at the idea of selling their interview, you can say that instead of offering them money, you'll let them sell their own interview, too.

Fourth, develop your list of questions. Have one big idea in mind that you want to make sure they cover. Focus on one topic and flesh out that topic completely.

However, be willing to leave your preplanned questions behind if the expert throws out an interesting tip or trick. Throw the question sheet away and ask for more information. Keep the conversation flowing. The key is to get meaningful specifics.

When it comes to actually conducting the interview, live calls with an audience are best. If you can get them to agree, invite members or subscribers on the live call. When you've got an audience, you can open it up to questions at the end, and there's a good chance that they are going to ask questions that you didn't think about.

When it comes to recording the interview, you can use a free option called FreeConferenceCall.com or a premium option called VoiceText.com. Both of them will allow you to record, but VoiceText has an operator on the line, so if something technical goes wrong, they can fix it for you.

Use written interviews only as a last resort. You'll lose the audio component, so it's not as valuable a product. You also can't probe for more information based on their responses. Instead, you'll send them a list of questions and they'll just send back a list of responses. So make sure you are thorough with your questions.

Do One, Do All

Now that you know the four different ways to execute the publisher model, it's time to take action. If you don't have your own product, go to your panel of experts and interview them. Ask them to write an e-book that you'll publish for a royalty deal.

Whatever arrangements you can make with them, just do it. But get those products. You will make much more money as an inbox magazine publisher even if you have your own products to sell; there's no faster way to do that than as a publisher with the publisher model.

PART

VI

BIG OR SMALL, YOUR CHOICE

Knowing your numbers is a fundamental precept of business.
—*Bill Gates*

Individuals don't win in business, teams do.
—*Sam Walton*

20

Measuring by the Numbers: The More You Know, the More You Grow

To run and grow your business, you need to know about all your key metrics. If you want to become a great entrepreneur, executive, or business owner, you need to face the facts. If you don't face facts, you can't grow your business.

The immediate reaction of most people is something like, "Ah, metrics. Ah, numbers. That's so boring. I don't want to have to deal with that." If you're thinking that, do you realize that you can measure almost every aspect of your success by numbers? If you look at your bank account and it has $10 in it, guess what? You're not doing great in the finance arena. If you're 5′4″ and the scale says 250 pounds, you're not doing great in the health department, either. If you have been divorced eight times, the personal pillar of your life most likely needs some help as well.

As you can see, numbers are the key to understanding the success or failure of anything you do, especially your business. So key metrics are the numbers that help determine the health of your business not only for today, but also for the week, month, quarter, and year.

Daily Key Metrics

Every day, there are important numbers you should look at. That's why we say key metrics. We don't just say daily metrics; we say daily key metrics. Daily key metrics are simply the vital factors about the health of your business that you need to look at every day. The three daily key metrics and reports that correlate are:

- Cash (cash report)
- Subscriber counts (on/off report)
- Current marketing results (marketing report—by campaign)

You need to look at your cash report. This means you need to how much money comes in the door every day—not projected money or future sales, but how much actual cash comes into your bank account every day.

This is essential because, first, you need to know how much money you need to make every day just to break even. I call this the "keep your doors open" number. With this number, don't forget to give yourself a salary, but don't pick an arbitrary number. Arbitrary numbers are really dangerous.

The biggest mistake that most business owners make is to define their salary as whatever is left over at the end of the month. Depending on how your business is doing, you're likely to make two big mistakes.

First, you may not even pay yourself at all. Second, you may take too much money out of your business and not leave enough to keep your business running. If you pay yourself a fair and reasonable salary, then you'll be running your business the right way.

To Keep the Doors Open = Fixed Plus Variable Expenses

You have to know all your fixed expenses that happen on a regular basis. This means the cost or expense does not change with an increase or decrease in the number of goods or services produced. Fixed costs are expenses that must be paid by a company for its business.

These are the same expenses you have to deal with every week or every month, such as paying rent for office space, the cost to host your website, or the cost of your phone conference bridge. If you have any salaried employees, they would fall under this category as well.

Next, you have to know your approximate variable expenses that will fluctuate during the month, depending on the output of products and services. For example, one month you may hire a copywriter, but the next month you may not need his or her services, or you may purchase a large quantity of media advertising one month but not the next.

Costs in Action

Let's use a simple example (see Figure 20.1). First determine what your salary will be. You need to consider what's fair and reasonable and what you really need to live on. Be realistic. When you're just getting started, it's probably not practical to give yourself a salary of $1 million a year. If you have a full-time day job and you're spending just a few hours a week on setting up and running your own inbox magazine, an annual salary of $50,000 is pretty good.

Let's say your annual fixed expenses are $6,000, which can include your autoresponder, utilities, rent, and other necessary expenses for running your business. That means you're paying $500 a month.

When you first get started, your autoresponder bill will cost the same every month. When your list gets much bigger, you'll start paying on a per-deployment basis. For now, you can mail about 10,000 people for $39 dollars a month. So your e-mail bill will be a fixed expense until you get a much larger list. Then your autoresponder bill will become a variable expense.

Cash Report: The Formula

- Your annual salary = $50,000

- Annual fixed expenses = $6,000
  (autoresponder, hosting, utilities, rent, etc.)

- Annual variable expenses = $12,000
  (marketing costs, freelancers, etc.)

- Total annual expenses = $68,000

Figure 20.1   Creating a cash report for your business.

Let's assume that your annual variable expenses are $12,000. I'm assuming you're buying media and paying freelancers a couple hundred dollars a month to do various work. Add up your salary ($50,000) with your fixed expenses ($6,000) and your variable expenses ($12,000) and you've got total annual expenses of $68,000 a year.

Divide $68,000 by 365, which represents the number of days in a year. So to keep your doors open, you need to make a $186.30 a day, which seems very reasonable. I didn't use a five-day workweek because your business will be earning money seven days a week. Remember, the biggest aspect of that equation is what you're paying yourself.

Now you can plug in different numbers and see what you can afford. If you decide to pay yourself $75,000 a year and your fixed and variable expenses remain the same, you'll know how much more you need to make every day.

In the beginning, as an entrepreneur, you'll need to sacrifice, such as putting in extra work because you know in the future your profits will be even bigger. You might be making $50,000 at your current job and give yourself a salary of $40,000 from your inbox magazine business. If you quit your full-time job, you'll be making less money, but you'll have much more freedom working for yourself. As an entrepreneur, you can do whatever makes you comfortable.

If you need a $186 a day to break even and you start making $250 a day, you might be tempted to take that incremental revenue and pocket it. However, if you're looking to really build something special, take any profit money and bank it.

Subscribers Are Your Lifeline

Another report is the daily on/off report that you can use to track the size of your subscriber list, how many people have joined that day, and how many people have unsubscribed that day (see Figure 20.2).

Suppose on May 1, your list contains 12,322 names. Then through media buys, joint ventures, viral PDFs, or any number of sources, 225 people opt in to your list. Now every day some people will unsubscribe, so let's say 21 people drop off your list. Because of your daily on/off report, you know that starting on May 2, you'll have 12,526 names on your subscriber list.

Daily On/Off Report

Date: <u>May 1, 2011</u>

List Size: <u>12,322</u>
\+ New Ons: <u>225</u>
\- New Offs: <u>21</u>
New Total: <u>12,526</u>

Figure 20.2   An example of a daily on/off report.

Business owners often focus on the new people added to their list, but they don't understand why their subscriber list isn't growing. That's because they're too focused on the addition and forget about the subtraction. It doesn't matter if you added 500 new names if you lose an equal number of names every day because then your list remains stagnant. More important, you aren't addressing the root cause of why people or failing off your list.

You need to look at your daily on/off report because your list is your greatest asset, and your greatest assets should always be tracked every day.

As you collect data from your daily on/off reports, you'll see how your list fluctuates on different days. If you added only 225 new names when you usually add 500 a day, you need to find out what might have happened. Maybe you had a technical glitch, such as your hosting servers not working, but you'll never know unless you're checking your on/off report every day. Or perhaps an affiliate who said they would mail their entire list only mailed a small portion.

What if you suddenly see a big spike in people unsubscribing from your list? You should check what you did in your last e-mail. Did you somehow insult your list? Did you use foul or offensive language? Perhaps the product or service you offered seemed slimy. Any time you see a big surge up or down, that's when you know you need to find out why. If it is a surge upward, you can quickly duplicate your success. If it is a surge downward, you must quickly fix the problem.

As a general rule, if more than 2 percent of your list unsubscribes per month, then something's wrong. You're either getting too many untargeted subscribers who should never have signed up to your list in the first place, or you're not treating them correctly.

You Can Improve Only if You Know Your Results

A few years ago, a young marketing assistant told me about a marketing campaign that her company had just launched. When I asked her how the campaign did, her enthusiastic reply was "fantastic." When I asked her specific questions about the campaign, her smile disappeared and she confessed they had not tracked the campaign. Naturally, I asked her why she thought it had done so well. Her reply was that the copy was great, so it had to have done well.

Unfortunately, this is the way many marketing assistants, managers, directors, and even entrepreneurs think. If you do not know the results of each specific element of a marketing campaign, your business will never grow and you will lose the same money over and over.

However, if you look at your active campaigns each day, you will see the winning elements, the elements that are making money, and roll out with your next campaign quickly. Remember, money loves speed!

Since different elements are often tracked in many different reports for different off-the-shelf customer relation management systems (CRMs), I find it easiest to simply to build this report in an Excel spreadsheet and duplicate it for each campaign. This way, you can just plug in the different results.

These are the elements you need to track and the report you need to build (see Figures 20.3 through 20.5). First, write down the campaign name, which is basically your product and offer. For this example, the product and offer is called the SIP-SqueezePage.

Next, write down the media and segment. In this example, the media is Newsmax and the segment is their progressive list, as opposed to their main list or expired list.

Third is the number of recipients, which means how many e-mails you sent for this campaign. Fourth, record the date that you ran the campaign. Fifth refers to the channel or the tactic of how people received your campaign, whether it was a dedicated e-mail

Marketing Report: Elements

1. Campaign name (product + offer)
   ex.: SIP-SqueezePage or SIP-SalesPage
2. Media and segment
   ex.: Newsmax—Progressive
3. Number of recipients
4. Run date
5. Channel (ex.: dedicated, co-reg, PPC, etc.)
6. CPM
7. Total cost

Figure 20.3   The elements of a marketing report.

Marketing Report (cont.)

8. Total opens (e-mail only)
9. Clicks
10. Click-through rate
11. Open rate (e-mail only)
12. Leads
13. Opt-in rate
14. Total sales (units)
15. Conversion rate

Figure 20.4   More elements of a marketing report.

or a banner ad. Sixth is the CPM, which stands for cost per thousand. Even though you already have a total cost, knowing your CPM lets you know how much it will cost to reach a larger or different quantity of names. Seventh is your total cost.

Eighth is your open total. This refers to an e-mail campaign and tells you how many people actually opened your e-mail message, which will always be less than the actual number of e-mails you sent out. If not many people are opening your e-mail messages, then you need to find out why. Perhaps your subject line was not interesting or engaging, or maybe there was a technical problem. Regardless, find out why.

Ninth are clicks. Your clicks tell you how many people clicked on your link to get to your squeeze page or sales page. Tenth is click-through rate. This is a calculation using the number of clicks received divided by the number of opens generated. A good benchmark for your inbox magazine is to have at least a 20 percent click-through rate. This tells you your list is engaged in the promotional copy and wants to read more.

Eleventh is the open rate. This is a calculation using the number of e-mails sent divided by the number of e-mails opened. This is important because you should always be striving for the 10 to 20 percent benchmark. If your open rate falls below the 10 percent mark, you may be sending too many promotions or content that your list does not find useful.

Twelfth are your leads. This tracks how many people visited your squeeze page and signed up for your offer. Thirteenth is opt-in rate, which tracks how many of those people actually signed up to subscribe to your inbox magazine. This is a calculation that takes the number of clicks divided by the number of leads. A good benchmark for an opt-in rate is 40 percent, especially for a free report.

Fourteenth is your total sales. This lets you now how many products or units you sold. Fifteenth is your conversion rate. This lets you know what percentage of people visiting your squeeze page who signed up.

With every campaign, you'll get the majority of your responses right away, but you'll still get responses up to three months after you've ended that particular campaign. That's why number 16, money collected (banked), and number 17, net sales (booked), are important elements on your marketing report.

Let's say you're selling a product that requires two payments of $97 dollars. If you made 10 sales, the money collected would be $970 dollars.

Since the total sale requires two payments, a certain percentage of people won't make that second payment. So every $97 customer might actually be worth an average of $168. For the net sales column, you'd make $1,680.

Finally, ROI stands for return on investment. To calculate ROI, take the total sales (this is your gross revenue) and divide by the

Marketing Report (cont.)

16. Money collected ("banked")
17. Net sales ("booked")
18. ROI (%)

Figure 20.5   More reporting elements.

total cost. This will give you a picture of how much money you have in the bank and lets you know whether to either continue the campaign at a faster pace or cut your losses.

This may seem daunting at first, but the beauty is that you have to build this report only once. Then, after that, you can use it for as long as you are in business!

Weekly Key Metrics

First of all, the fact that you need to look at certain weekly key metrics doesn't mean that you stop looking at your daily metrics. Your daily metrics tell you what's happening to your business every day. Your weekly metrics are different because they tell you if your business is on track for whatever goals you may be pursuing.

There are three weekly key metrics you need to look at:

- Month-to-date revenue
- Marketing calendar
- Project status report

Revenues by Month

Your month-to-date revenue report tracks your total revenues in the current month (see Figure 20.6). If this is your first week of the month and its June 7, your month-to-date revenue metric will track the revenue that came in from June 1 through June 7.

You need to itemize this by campaign and make sure you track every campaign. You need to see how each campaign functions so you can see if they're meeting your assumptions.

Next, you need to subtract your variable costs, which are things like refunds, affiliate commissions, marketing costs, and merchant fees. You also need to subtract all fixed costs for your overhead. The goal of this report is to have positive cash flow by the end of the first week of each month.

Don't forget that you can make your variable and fixed costs part of your weekly key metrics, such as counting them for only a quarter of the month. Instead of the start of every month listing $5,000 for your entire monthly rent, each week you just list your rent as $1,250.

Other people like starting out each month with all of their fixed and variable costs listed. That shows you how much you have to earn back in the next three weeks to come out ahead. If you can break even by the end of that first week with all your expenses factored in, then you'll know you've got a very healthy business.

When you come to the end of that first week and all of your bills are paid, then you can focus the rest of the month on making money. Now you can make strategic, long-term decisions.

Month-to-Date Revenue Report

- **Total revenues—MTD** (itemized by campaign).

- **Subtract variable costs** (ex. refunds, affiliate commissions, marketing costs, merchant fees, etc.).

- **Subtract fixed costs** (overhead).

GOAL: Go positive by end of first week of each month!

Figure 20.6   The parts of a month-to-date revenue report.

Mark Your Calendar

The next report is a marketing calendar. This could be a Google calendar in any format that you like, but make sure you print it out. Your marketing calendar should have a rolling four-week cycle, with at least two weeks set in stone and the remaining two weeks being more flexible.

A common mistake is to plan out the marketing calendar for the whole month, such as deciding what promotions to have and how to execute it for the entire month. At the end the month, companies often wonder what to do next month?

A better way is to use a rolling four-week cycle so that by the second week of the month, you already know what to do for the third and fourth week of the month.

Meet on a scheduled day and time each week to discuss the following week's calendar. Personally, I like Thursdays because by Thursday afternoon you know what's going on for the following week and what your results have been thus far. When you start Monday morning, nobody asks, "What are we doing this week?"

Many companies hold Monday morning meetings, which is a big waste of time. Monday morning should be your most productive time, so don't burn through it just trying to figure out your week. By the end of the week, you should pretty much know what's happening on Friday. So in your Thursday afternoon meeting, talk about the following Monday through Friday.

For your marketing calendar, use the first week of the month for a big in-house promotion, and each of the following weeks for affiliate swaps. Use that first week to get that big money in. Start it off right. Then you know by that third week if you need to go back to an in-house promotion or stay with your affiliate swaps. The goal is to break even by that first week, and that involves making sure that you've got a big promotion ready to roll that first week of each month.

With in-house promotions, you're not paying anything out so the money goes into your bank account today. With affiliate promotions, you make may make plenty of sales, but you have to wait for your affiliate check. Until that check comes in, you can't count it as part of your revenue report. You may need to adjust the calendar based on your month-to-date revenue report.

Suppose the first big promotion that you do is to launch a new product or start a new service on the first week of August, and it bombs. If you had planned your rolling four-week calendar based on your big promotion going well, you'll suddenly need to schedule some other promotions. Some may be for other people and some may be for other in-house products.

The opposite can also happen where you have an offer or promotion that exceeds your expectations and you expected to run it for only one week, but you keep mailing for two more weeks because it's making so much money. If you're going to change your marketing calendar, the only real acceptable reason to change it is that the month-to-date revenues are "telling" you to do so, not because of missed deadlines.

The three marketing calendar items you need include:

- House e-mails
- Media buys
- Affiliate promotions

House e-mails include anything you're selling of your own. It can be sending out an inbox magazine issue or a promotion. Always track what you're mailing out to your own list on a calendar.

Media buys let you track the number of new names your promotions will be going to. The results of these buys will be reflected on your on/off report. That way, you can see how everything you're doing is affecting your subscriber list.

With affiliate promotions, make sure that if you have promised something to someone, then you get it done. Also, if someone else is mailing for you, you want to keep track of that.

To help you keep track of so many different types of mailings, color-code them on your marketing calendar. You might color house e-mails in black, media buys in red, and affiliate promotions in green. With affiliate promotions, you may need to use different colors as well. That way you can see who is mailing for you and who you are mailing for.

Now, at a glance, you can see if you're not sending out enough e-mails. You should be mailing to your own list at least three to four times per week. You should have mailings for your list to grow (affiliates and media buys) at least the same amount. Your marketing calendar is one of your best management tools that you have.

Your Status, Please

Next, you need a project status report (see Figure 20.7). Everybody talks about the ideas they want to do that will produce revenue, but they don't track them. So many business entrepreneurs fall into the bright and shiny syndrome, where they pursue the latest interesting project and lose track of their current projects.

The best way to avoid the bright and shiny syndrome is to make sure you have a project status report. Suppose I have an idea and start working on a new product. It's great that I'm 50 percent done, but then I get a better idea, so I start on that one until it, too, is 50 percent done.

Pretty soon I've got five projects that are each 50 percent done. Guess what? Five projects that are only 50 percent done will yield zero revenue. One project that's 100 percent done will yield revenue. That's why a project status report is so important.

I like to build this in Excel as well, but there are plenty of project management solutions you can purchase. If you do this, make sure everyone uses the same tool. I prefer to build my own project management tool because then it has every line item I need.

First, every item on a project status report needs a title. Next, put a task on there. The task might be to write a lead magnet. Then define who will actually get that task done. Essentially, who's the person responsible, the champion?

Project Status Report

- **Project title** (ex.: "40 Days and 40 Nights")

- **Task** (ex.: Write lead magnet)

- **Champion** (ex.: Craig)

- **Original due date** (ex.: May 28, 2011)

- **Status** (ex.: Completing research, on target, interviewing, waiting for feedback, writing body copy, completed, etc.)

- **Revised due date** (ex.: N/A, June 15, 2011)

  IMPORTANT: Each TASK gets its own line item!!

Figure 20.7   The elements of a project status report.

Track the original due date on which you want that task done. Finally, note the status of that task. You might be writing a lead magnet, completing research, interviewing an expert, waiting for feedback, or writing body copy. These are examples of specific statuses of tasks.

Every week, you update the statuses of each project so you'll know how fast it's progressing and approximately when it might be completed. You might list multiple tasks under a given project and assign different champions to accomplish each task. If tasks aren't getting done on time, you might have to create a revised due date. A great example for a revised due date would be N/A, which stands for not applicable. A revised due date lets you know if a project is slipping and by how much. If you aren't launching a product on the day you expected, you can't expect to have that money in the bank when you thought you would.

It's easy to start a project and literally let six months to a year go by without tracking its progress. If you are maintaining a project status report, you can see how much the revised due date differs from the original due date. Never modify that original due date.

If you look at your project status report and see a bunch of N/As running down on the revised due date side, that means you're hitting your targets. Not only are you doing a great job of estimating how long tasks will take, you're completing them on time. If you are constantly revising the due dates for your projects, that means there's something broken somewhere in your business.

Pretty soon, you'll be able to spot patterns. Maybe Bob keeps falling behind on his projects, while Greg never misses a deadline. By studying your weekly project status report, you can see who's doing what they're supposed to be doing and who isn't.

Your weekly project status report needs to be task-centric. Every major task requires that a whole lot of little tasks get done. If you break them down on a per-task basis and assign them, then you'll know what needs to be done and who needs to do it at any given time.

Ideally, you need a single point of accountability for every task on a project status report. If somebody keeps missing deadlines, you'll be able to identify that person. Without a weekly project status report, you'll never know what's happening or why nothing seems to be getting done.

Long-Term Metrics

Besides daily and weekly key metrics, you also need to manage longer-range metrics. That includes monthly profit-and-loss statements (P&Ls), quarterly employee reviews, and a yearly post mortem. A P&L tracks all the money coming in and going out. It's important that you scrutinize every line at least once a month so you know where your money is going.

Ideally, you should use bookkeeping software, such as QuickBooks, starting from day one. QuickBooks is easy to use and there's a lot of free training out there. You need to understand every line that you put in your P&L, and you need to scrutinize those lines every month (see Figure 20.8).

Once you start making about $10,000 a month, you should invest in an outsourced bookkeeper. It won't cost you a lot of money and will save you time. Paying a bookkeeper might seem like an unnecessary expense, but you may be hemorrhaging cash and not know it. Your bookkeeper will pay for him- or herself just by catching careless mistakes with your bank or affiliate over payments.

When you start making about $100,000 a month, bring your bookkeeping in house. You'll have enough money to make sure it's worth it. This will save money, so you can make even more money at this point.

Next are employee evaluation forms (see Figure 20.9). Many people think you need to do an employee evaluation only once

Profit-and-Loss Statement

- Scrutinize every single line at least once a month!

- Should use bookkeeping software (i.e., QuickBooks) starting Day 1!!!

- Hire an outsourced bookkeeper once you're making over $10,000 a month.

- Bring accounting in-house when you hit $100,000-a-month mark.

Figure 20.8   Criteria for using a profit-and-loss statement.

Employee Evaluation Forms

- **Filled out by the direct supervisors**, and helps determine…

- **Do they know what they do?** (What's their job description and has it changed?)

- **Do they know their personal monthly/quarterly/ yearly goals?** (i.e., key metrics and major projects)

- **Have they improved since the last review?**

- **Are they suited for the job they're in, or is it time to make a change?** (i.e., career development)

Figure 20.9   The purpose of an employee evaluation form.

a year, but I recommend that you do this quarterly. An employee evaluation form needs to be filled out by the employee's direct supervisor. This form will help determine the following:

- Does the employee know what she does and actually understand what her job is? Business constantly evolves, so someone's position will change over time, even if she has the same title. Duties and responsibilities will be added, and some things will go onto other people. So make sure the person knows what she's doing.
- Does the employee understand her personal monthly, quarterly, and yearly goals? Does she understand the key metrics and major projects that she is responsible for? You cannot hold people accountable if they don't know what they're supposed to do.
- Has the employee improved since her last review? Is she even suited for this job, or is it time to make a change? Is there a clear career development, career advancement path?

Next is the yearly postmortem. For me, this is one of the most fun days at the office. Actually, I make this into a two- or three-day postmortem because you need to go over the entire year and all the campaigns you launched, and not just celebrate your successes. You also need to look at your failures to make sure you learn from them and don't repeat them.

A postmortem is really about the strategic vision of your company, because your company is evolving and your vision will change. It might be slight or it might be major, but you need to make sure that everybody in the company understands the strategic vision.

You need to talk about the numbers regarding each individual campaign. If you're running several different inbox magazines, you'll need to focus on each one individually.

During this strategic vision period, you might decide to launch a new inbox magazine. You might decide that your strategic vision of your company is that you're not just a financial company. Instead of focusing exclusively on stocks, maybe you'll branch out into currencies as well or even talk about alternative health.

Just make sure that your decisions are made with your strategic vision in mind and not done willy-nilly. Besides making sure all your people understand your strategic vision, make sure the financial numbers can support your vision, too.

You also need to look at your products. Never fall in love with a product to a point where you can't say, "Our strategic vision doesn't support this product anymore, and the numbers don't support this product anymore."

You might need to cancel that product and get rid of it if it's not a part of your company's mission anymore. If your strategic vision and company change, you most likely need to say, "We need to add new products."

So you need to examine your strategic vision, your numbers, and your product line. At General Electric, every year they got rid of any employee they rated as a C player. That meant they literally fired 20 percent of their people to get rid of the worst 20 percent. Regardless of your relationship with any particular people, you need to make sure they are right for your vision, meet the numbers, create the products, and market the products.

This is all driven from your strategic vision. You'll often have good people who helped you get to your current level, but if you want to grow, you'll have certain people who can't take you to that next level.

That's when you need to decide that if someone is a good bookkeeper, but he can't be the chief financial officer, you need to bring someone else on board as his boss. Even if someone's the head of a division or a department, he's going to have to accept the fact that someone new might be a boss over him.

You may decide from a strategic vision standpoint that a certain product might be fine since it is making money, but the person that you publish is difficult with a big ego, and so maybe you should just set that one aside and spend those resources elsewhere.

The only way to have a great company is to have the right people in the right positions. If you don't, you can have great vision and great ideas, but if you don't have the right people, you won't succeed. On the flip side, when you have great people doing the right things, everything is so much easier.

Of course, you also have to look at how everything gets done. Do your procedures still work? If not, why? Throughout the year, your procedures should evolve. Steps should have been added or changed because nothing should be just okay. Nothing should be just good enough.

You should never have the attitude that a procedure works okay when you can always make it better. Maybe you'll need to add or remove steps to make a procedure work more efficiently.

Examining your business and your people isn't that crucial when you're just getting started because you are mostly doing everything, but you need to plan ahead. When you grow into a multimillion-dollar company, it will matter and you'll need to take these issues seriously in order to keep growing.

Successful Entrepreneurs Love Numbers

For so long, the "numbers" element on business has a gotten a bad reputation, when in reality it is one of the easiest and most enjoyable areas to manage. It is also the area of business that serious entrepreneurs care about. And when you break it down into simple, direct, concise reporting, it becomes that much easier. You will find that once you decide to take these reports seriously, they will help your business grow.

All you need to do is copy the reports that I have provided for you and start plugging in your numbers, even if you are the one preparing them. The great news is that in the next chapter, we talk about building your team. So once you have a great understanding of these reports, you will be doing the actual preparation of them until you hire your first employee.

21

Building Your Team: It's Good to Be Great!

I n case you don't know who Peter Drucker is, he's probably one of the greatest business strategists ever to have lived. He said that most entrepreneurs fail because they don't know their strengths. That means that you identify your strengths as an entrepreneur and build on those strengths.

People think they should only work on their weaknesses, but that's not true. What you need to do is find people who enhance your strengths and who can do what you're not good at. Then and only then can you turn what you are good at into greatness.

Regardless which company I was running at the time and regardless of the total number of employees, I never had more than six to seven direct reports (people reporting directly to me) plus an assistant. My direct reports ran individual departments and never had more than seven direct reports. As a general rule, you should never have more than seven direct reports because as the CEO (or any management position), you simply cannot manage more than seven people effectively.

I have consulted for organizations that literally had a flat line organization where twenty people (or more) reported to a single person. That's just not effective. No one can effectively manage that many people. All you are doing at that point are setting your employees up for failure and soon your company will collapse.

When I started my inbox magazine of Working Moms Only .com, I had been in the corporate world my entire life. In some companies I had 30 employees, others up to 200 (see Figure 21.1).

ORGANIZATION CHART:

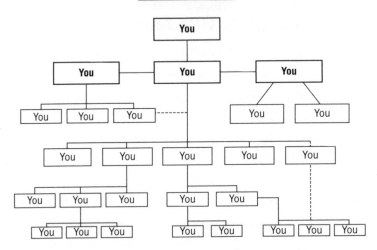

Figure 21.1   My first organizational chart running Working Moms Only.

Now suddenly, I realized that by running my own business, I was doing everything.

I went back to that Peter Drucker quote and recognized what my strengths were, and what I wasn't either particularly good at or what I didn't like to do. That's how I started outsourcing and/or hiring people. When you're first getting started, this is where you'll be doing everything yourself. However, if you want to grow, you'll have to rely on other people.

You may be thinking that if you're just one person, you don't need an organizational chart, but you actually do. For now, your organizational chart will look like you are doing everything, but you need to identify tasks within your company that you want to get rid of as soon as possible.

When I started out, I actually did have writers who were working for me, and guess who they were? They were my expert panelists. When you start off, you actually do have an organizational chart full of other people.

Who and When

So who do you hire and when?

When you hit $10,000 a month, that's the time to hire your first employee (see Figure 21.2). Start with your biggest problem. Is

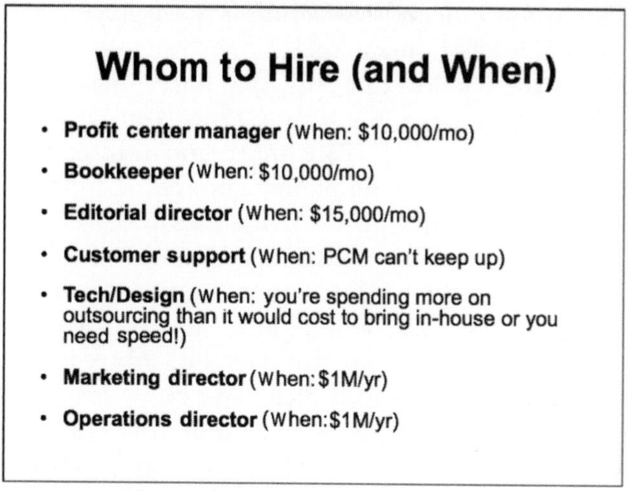

Whom to Hire (and When)

- **Profit center manager** (When: $10,000/mo)

- **Bookkeeper** (When: $10,000/mo)

- **Editorial director** (When: $15,000/mo)

- **Customer support** (When: PCM can't keep up)

- **Tech/Design** (When: you're spending more on outsourcing than it would cost to bring in-house or you need speed!)

- **Marketing director** (When: $1M/yr)

- **Operations director** (When: $1M/yr)

Figure 21.2   When to hire people.

bookkeeping your biggest challenge? Maybe you really need help marketing and running your business. That's why having an organizational chart in place is important, because you'll want to start plugging names into these boxes.

The first person that you will most likely need and want to hire is a profit center manager. When do you do this? When you're making around $10,000 a month. Basically, a profit center manager maximizes the revenues of your marketing campaigns.

When a marketing campaign is working, they need to take it to the next level by finding more affiliate partners, more media to buy and more joint venture partners. They need to understand every line in your profit and loss statements. This is the person who puts together your marketing calendar and project status reports, and analyzes your current marketing reports. They will also serve as your customer service representative in the beginning. If they are doing their job correctly, they will pay for themselves within their first 30 days of employment.

Next, you need to hire a bookkeeper when you start earning $10,000 a month. This is the person who makes all the entries in your profit and loss statements every month. They will also pay all your invoices and keep track of affiliate payments coming in and going out of the organization. At this point, this bookkeeper could be an outsourced bookkeeper. You can have this person in-house;

however they will not need to be a full time employee. At this point they can work 15 to 20 hours a week.

When you are starting out and only have one or two employees, a virtual environment is just fine. Once you have six or more full time employees, getting office space and bringing them all in house will most likely serve you better. The reason for this is simple; you want cohesiveness and productivity. This is better served when the entire team understands each other's functions.

You may be considering hiring an editorial director when you're making at least $15,000 a month, especially if you have multiple inbox magazines. Let's say you have two inbox magazines that publish twice a week. That's four issues a week.

An editorial director makes sure that the editorial content meets your editorial guidelines and remains an advocate for your subscribers. He or she also needs to keep your readers engaged. They're the person who puts the inbox magazine together and, depending on your niche, does any fact checking. They also work very closely with the profit center manager to make sure the ad selections within your inbox magazine are synergistic with the content.

The best part about having an editorial director is that he or she can still outsource your content. Your expert panelists are an example of outsourced content writing. If you want someone to write a special report or a lead magnet, outsource the task, especially if it's just a temporary job.

You will need to hire a dedicated customer service representative when your profit center manager cannot keep up with the volume. Here's a little rule of thumb: for every customer complaint that you receive, there are 33 people who feel the exact same way but just didn't take the time to let you know.

Remember, we said that everything can be measured by numbers. If 10 people complain about one of your products or services, that's not just 10 people complaining. That's 10 people multiplied by 33. So instead of thinking only 10 had a problem with your product, the real number is 330. That's a lot of customers who have a problem with a product or your company. If you or your profit center manger can't keep up with making good on these complaints, you're losing money.

You should follow up with all complaints within 24 hours. That's when you know if your customer support is doing its job. If people have to wait more than 48 hours to get a call back or an e-mail, that's when you know they have fallen behind because nobody should have to wait that long.

Next, let's talk about your technical and design needs. When you are spending more on outsourcing than what it would cost to bring a full time person in house, you need to hire someone. This is an issue about speed. When you have sales copy written but don't have someone to design and put it together on a sales page, is the worst feeling in the world.

When you're starting out or even when you're making $25,000 to $50,000 a month, you might only need one of these people with occasional outsourcing. Outsourcing is about speed. Just because you have a skilled employee in house does not mean you can't outsource an occasional project.

Now you may wonder where you should outsource some of these projects. Graphic design is pretty easy to outsource through sites like eLance, oDesk, and 99designs. Technology is another easy task to outsource. You don't need an information technology (IT) department when you're just starting out.

The Million-Dollar Mark

When you hit this pivotal number, things really start to change. When you start making more than a million dollars a year, that's when you need to hire a few people at a "director level." These are folks who will have people reporting directly to them, so that you are dealing with few of the details and concentrating on the big picture. Once you have director level employees in place, your job is more about outside deal making and idea generation.

One of the director level positions you will need is a marketing director. This is the person who will eventually be managing your profit center managers, because at a million dollars a year, chances are good that you probably have more than one profit center manager.

A marketing director can help you with your vision and media buys along with being a leader in your organization. When you hire a marketing director, you never ever want to hire somebody who has worked in an advertising agency on branding.

What we have been talking about this entire time is direct response marketing, which is the kind of marketing that is specific, quantifiable, and immediate. So you want a marketing director who has direct response marketing experience. This person will also manage your copywriters and designers.

You also need an operations director when you start making a million dollars a year. When you are starting out and have a profit center manager, they will do a little operations and marketing.

Marketing is directly responsible for generating revenue. Operations may do things like negotiating the lease for your rent, setting up your merchant account, setting up your IT system, or even managing payroll.

Operations people can save you a lot of money by taking obnoxious burdens away from the creative people so they can continue to bring money in the door and making sure that you keep as much money as possible. Marketing people work to create as much money as possible. Don't confuse those two tasks since they require the skills of very different people.

Copywriting is something that you should never outsource completely. It is best to have at least one to two good copywriters in house with an outsourced stable of copywriters available at any time.

In almost all the companies I have worked for as a CEO, president, or consultant, there was a direct correlation between the amount of money spent on copywriting and the success of the company. So when you find a great copywriter, hold on to them at all costs.

Having a great copywriter and a great marketing director together is the one combination of employees that will increase the success of your business the fastest. You need to make sure that they have chemistry and mutual respect for each other.

Never, Never, Never Outsource . . .

What you should never outsource is your strategic vision. That always needs to come from you and your partner, even people within the organization who care and love your organization.

Having said that, there is nothing wrong with bringing people in to help you brainstorm, but the strategic vision must be yours. Don't be swayed or enamored by something you see someone else execute. High back to why you started your company and stay true to your mission and values.

Also, do not outsource your marketing strategy. Your marketing strategy will include your hooks and offers that you develop for your promotional pieces. This means the big idea behind the campaign and what your customers will receive when they purchase. This should come from your team.

You should know better than any outsider who your customer is and what your subscribers like. You've done all that research and tested your own ideas along with running affiliate promotions. If you just hand this vital task to somebody else, then you are going to get back something that's going to like trying to jam a square peg into a round hole.

Never outsource your media buying. This would be like handing someone your checkbook and saying, "Do what you want." Agencies will charge you on what you spend, not on your results. This is why it's crucial that somebody in your organization understands how to buy media. When you are spending big money, you need to control this.

Remember, I am saying no agencies; I am not saying no list brokers because list brokers aid you. They may make recommendations but remember, you're the one writing the checks. You still need to be making the final decision on what you purchase.

This will be very clear when you are talking to an agency person and the first question they ask is, "What's your marketing and advertising budget?"

That's when you know you are dealing with an agency mindset. Because if you tell them that your budget is $100,000, they'll take a check from you for $100,000, put $15,000 to $20,000 in their pocket, and then start spending your money using their supposed expertise. When you're a big company like Coca-Cola and you're doing a branding campaign, maybe that approach will work. For you as a direct response marketer, don't use agencies.

This means that you are always controlling what you are spending your money on. No one else should be doing this. You need to go through every invoice and every insertion order. Never hand over your checkbook to someone else because this is how people lose money.

Gross Revenue versus Profits

People like to brag about gross revenue, but gross revenue is meaningless. Any moron can build a million dollar company if you give him $2 million. What's important is the money you put in the bank. You don't bank gross revenue; you only put profits in the bank.

Still, many entrepreneurs gauge their success by this factor. But in reality the only success factor you should be looking at are your profits. This is why you really need to decide what your goals are.

I once had a client tell me that they wanted a $25 million company. When I asked him why, he said because that would be cool.

To me, that is a ridiculous answer.

Decide on your profit goal first and work your way backwards. This will determine how many customers you need, which will directly correlate to the number of employees you need to hire.

As you grow there will come a time when you can't be as involved in the day to day operations of your business, so you'll need someone else to write a check when you're out of town. However, in the beginning, nobody writes a check and nobody approves a major expense over a fixed amount such as $500 dollars.

When the time comes that you have grown to a $2 to $3 million company, you will need to have a Chief Financial Officer (CFO) in house. This is someone who comes with great references and you trust completely. That's because that person will start paying the bills and signing the checks, but only once the proper standard operating procures (SOP) are in place. One of those SOPs will be you meeting with your CFO on a weekly basis and going through payables and receivables. Your CFO will always report to the CEO.

Don't forget, when you give someone that kind of authority, it works both ways. With authority comes accountability. It may be somebody you trust, but never go without spot-checking. Make sure everyone is held accountable for what they do.

The example organizational chart in Figure 21.3 should be used for companies ranging in size from about $10 million dollars to about $30 million. As you can see, the organizational chart clearly emphasizes that the director level positions are department heads. You can also see that even in fairly large corporations, out-sourcing still makes sense.

I like to use a metric for every full time employee you have, you should be making about $500,000 to $1 million in revenue. In the beginning, you might be making $250,000 to $500,000 per employee, but your eventual goal should be $1 million per

Example Organizational Chart

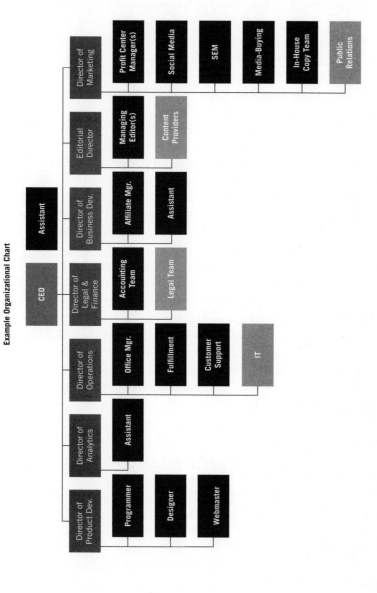

Figure 21.3 The parts of a typical organization.

employee. That's when you'll know your business is healthy and when you can afford to hire even more people if necessary.

Remember, starting out, you may not actually have a director of marketing because it will be you. You're going to be most of those top level positions. You might have a profit center manager, but it's unlikely that you are going to have your own social media team, search engine marketing team, and media buying team right in the beginning.

The boxes that are asterisked (*) represent jobs that are typically outsourced even when talking about $20 or $30 million company. At this size you don't even need an in house IT department because you can outsource a company that comes in a few times month to make sure everything is all right.

You (in most cases) do not need in-house lawyers. Having a firm on retainer that specializes in your niche will most likely be your most cost effective solution.

When you look at this organizational chart, you'll see that there aren't more than seven people reporting to any one person. That's extremely important to keep from getting overwhelmed or allowing tasks to get lost.

Take organization seriously and create your own organizational chart, even if your name appears in every box. As your inbox magazine business grows, you'll be able to fill your chart with people to do the jobs you'd rather not do or that don't represent your core strengths.

A Good Problem to Have

"Sure," you may be thinking, "But I'm an idea person. The last thing I want to do is manage people." And that's ok. Actually it's great. Look, if you are reaching the benchmarks we described above, that means you are making good money. And if you are making good money, you can hire someone to manage your employees and run the operations of your business.

The last thing you want to do is stop the growth and momentum of your business because you don't want to manage people.

CHAPTER 22

Positioning for the Sale: Your Big Payday

How can you position your inbox magazine for sale? Right now this might seem crazy, especially if you're just starting your inbox magazine. How can you even imagine selling it one day?

Owning a business is much like owning a boat. The joke is that the best two days of a boat owner's life are the day he buys a boat and the day he sells it. Whether that's your goal or not, whether you think this might be your eventual goal, it's still important to know. The tasks you need to position your inbox magazine for sale are the same tasks you need to create for a successful inbox magazine so you can enjoy your life and freedom.

There are really two types of buyers of any business. First are investors, which include venture capital firms, mergers and acquisition firms, private equity groups, and high-net-worth individual investors. These are the types of people who will buy your company even if they don't know much about it. That's because they want to flip it to somebody else for more money, or they just want it for passive income.

The second type of buyer is a strategic buyer, who might be a direct or indirect competitor. He may be somebody in a similar market but he really wants to get into yours. He may already be doing something similar and want to expand or grow by acquiring other businesses.

You might be thinking that the best deal will be to sell your business to others who are in business with you, but in reality, the bigger money usually happens when you sell to that first group, the investor group. But the only way that will happen is if your business is structured well.

Strategic deals can happen between rivals, but strategic buyers will rarely be able to pay you the type of money that an investor can. If you deliberately position your company for investors, you will have a head start on the process when the time comes to sell.

Getting Ready

The first way to maximize your sale is to increase your earnings before interest, taxes, depreciation, and amortization (EBITDA). It's a fancy accountant phrase that basically means your net income (see Figure 22.1). How much money did you actually make? How much money fell to the bottom line after accounting for every expense, including your salary?

When you're selling your business, your business value will be some multiple of that EBITDA number. If you're using QuickBooks or a bookkeeper, you should be able to calculate this number quickly and easily. The more money you make, the more money you can sell your company for.

Another factor that determines the value of your business is more intangible by the systems that you have in place, which are your standard operating procedures (SOPs). If you wake up every

---

Maximizing the Sale

1. **Increase EBITDA.**

2. **Have systems in place** (SOPs).

3. **Have predictable, repeatable income**
   (regular advertisers, subscriptions,
   webinars, events, etc.).

Figure 22.1   The elements of maximizing your business for sale.

morning and you don't know what you're going to do today, you might have a good lifestyle business, but that is not a system, and nobody will be able to buy that.

You need to follow a number of SOPs—everything from hiring employees to generating reports that you need to track on a daily, weekly, monthly, quarterly, annually basis. These must be repeatable tasks that you need to follow for the business to produce revenue. Those are all systems.

The way that you grow your business or start up a new one is all about systems. Anybody who wants to buy your business will want to see how well your systems work. I like to call this "McDonaldizing" your business. When McDonald's trains new employees, they do so with SOPs in place. Every time McDonald's makes a Big Mac, they do it the exact same way. That same structure needs to go into your business.

If you have an e-mail system that consistently gets people to sign up and attend a webinar, and then predictably converts attendees into buying products, that's an SOP that people want to see.

So begin systemizing all your processes. Not only will this make you a more successful business owner, but it'll make you a more attractive purchase opportunity.

Another factor that makes your business more appealing is if it generates predictable, repeatable income. Nobody is going to buy a company that did $1 million one month and then goes another six months before it makes any more money. That's not predictable, repeatable income.

If you've got a successful inbox magazine, perhaps you have regular advertisers who may book space in your inbox magazine or website out for six months to a year in advance. That's good, and that's what investors want to see. That's predictable, repeatable income.

If you convert free subscribers to paid subscribers within 30 days with proven tactics, again that's what investors are looking for. Or if you've got a continuity business, such as a membership or a subscription business that shows predictable, repeatable income month after month after month, that's a concrete business. At that point, an investor knows that all he needs to do is to continue doing what you've been doing, and he should see the same results with the same kind of money coming in.

Events are also attractive to investors. If you can attract a large number of people to events time after time, investors see this as both a repeatable and predictive revenue stream. The best part is that they can be online events, such as webinars, or offline events, such as conferences or summits. As long as you can show that you make predictable, repeatable income, investors will see how they can make the same predictable, repeatable income.

Here's an example of an SOP used by Working Moms Only (WMO) that defines how to send large files.

WMO—YouSendIt.com SOP

YouSendIt.com is a website that is used for sending large-sized files that typically exceed standard e-mail service size limitations. Because you cannot send the large file itself, YouSendIt.com allows you to send a link to the file; the recipient can link to the file that is temporarily housed on the YouSendIt site.

1. Go to www.yousendit.com.
   a. Select "Login" on the main screen.

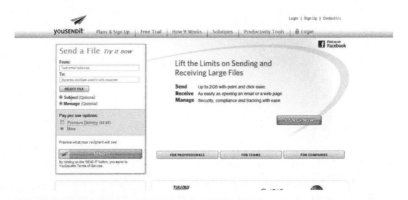

   b. Enter e-mail login and password, and click the "Login" button.

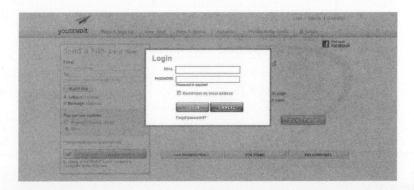

c. You will then be taken to the Overview screen.

d. Click the "Send Now" button.

e. You will go to the Send Files screen.

f. Enter the e-mail address, subject line, and any text you want to send along with the file.

g. Click the "Select File" button and browse to pick the file that you want to send.

h. Highlight the file and click the "Open" button.

i. The file name will now appear on the Send Files screen.

j. Click the "Send It" button.

k. The site will give you a progress report on the status of the file delivery.

l. An offer to receive a confirmation that the file is actually downloaded from the site for a fee will pop up; click the "No Thanks" button.

m. The recipient will receive an e-mail message that looks like the following:

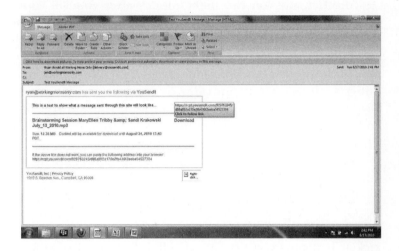

n. The account is currently set up to appear that files come from Ryan; this can be changed.

o. *Important note:* Files are available for download for only seven days (this is noted in the body of the e-mail to the recipient).

Good Things Come in Threes

When it comes to actually selling your company, there are three main ways that you can make money. First, you can earn a multiple of the EBITDA such as two to six times. Less than two means there is something wrong. Most likely, the business has not been run properly or your particular niche is faltering. A three or four times EBITDA is pretty common. If you are getting five or six times EBITDA then you are either making a lot of money or you're just doing something really special.

Just to put this into perspective, let's say you make $1 million a year net. That means that you could walk away with a pretty healthy check. There are a lot of reasons to take three times what you made. One reason is that you can always do it again. Or perhaps you want to sail around the world with your spouse or start a nonprofit organization. If you do want to start a new business that is similar to the last business you created, just make sure you don't sign a noncompete agreement forbidding you to do so.

Another way you can make money after you sell your business is by staying on and earning a consulting fee. You may not want to do this, but it could be a condition of the sale. Very often, such a condition is written into the agreement. If that is the case, negotiate a monthly retainer or even a salary. Make sure you identify your duties such as content provider or product development. You can also require a clause that states how long you will remain with the company. Anywhere from six months to three years is reasonable. This helps ensure that the transition is smooth.

Many people sell their business and wind up making as much in salary as they were running the business. Only now the responsibility of running the company does not fall on their shoulders.

Often, when you sell your company, you sell a majority interest in your company, but keep a portion, which is called an equity kicker. It means you do not sell off 100 percent of your company. The reason is that the buyer will still want you involved. Since you still have partial ownership in your business, you are vested in the success of the company.

There are many situations where the original business owners retain a fairly small equity kicker of 10 to 20 percent. But because the new owner can grow the business bigger and better, the original owner ends up making more money just from distributions than she did when she owned 100 percent of the business.

Unfortunately, there may be times when the new owner might destroy your business as well. That's why you want to get your check up front and decide how involved you want to be after the sale.

You typically need to run your business for at least three years before you can seriously consider selling it. After you've been running it for two years, it's not uncommon to start putting out feelers about selling your business, but potential buyers want to see about two to three years of consistent revenue and stability. Otherwise, you risk selling your business at a very low multiple.

You don't want to do that—not when you worked that hard. You want to put in the time and get the EBITDA you want, which usually takes about three years.

Start the Right Way

Just remember, having systems in place and having a predictable and repeatable income is what makes your business valuable and attractive to others. It's not about launches or promotions. It's about knowing how to make money month after month, year after year, so put those systems in place now and you'll be glad that you did.

Epilogue:
Still Growing Strong and Damn Proud

Running a business takes a lot of blood, sweat, and tears (and caffeine). But at the end of the day, you should be building something you will be proud of.

—Sir Richard Branson

Even though I had been applying pieces of the inbox magazine model we just discussed for years prior to starting my "first and own" inbox magazine, I still had to learn through trial and error.

I didn't have the kind of road map you now do to tell me what to do next. Through a lot of determination and a little bit of luck, I forced myself to learn enough to get started. I didn't know how to set up a website; I did not know how to deploy an e-mail. While running large companies, I always had someone else handle those kinds of tasks.

Every time I ran across another obstacle, self-doubt came into play. I thought I might have to give up, I might have to go back and work for someone else, but I didn't. I kept going. I kept asking questions. I kept talking to people who I thought might know the answers. If they didn't know the answer, they could often point me to someone who might know.

The reason for my success today is that I just never gave up and I never stopped learning. I wasn't any smarter than anyone else or better educated. I knew what I wanted to do and I kept figuring out how to reach my goal. It wasn't always easy or fun, but each time I overcame another obstacle, that gave me the confidence that I could keep moving forward and overcome the next barrier in my way.

That's why I wrote this book, to help clear the way for everyone else to set up their own inbox magazine with a whole lot less confusion, frustration, and pain than I had to go through. I've provided the guidance and given you the road map I wish someone had given me when I was just getting started. Now it's up to you. I have provided the information and the inspiration. It is up to you to provide the perspiration.

You can do it. It might take longer than you want, but you could surprise yourself and find that it takes far less time and effort than you might think. The only way to find out is to get started and see it through to the end.

Now that you've finished this book, keep it by your side as a reference. Each time you're ready to make the next step, you can review the chapter that covers that topic. The more times you re-read a chapter, the more times you'll uncover new information that you may have skipped over before or that you didn't think was important at the time. Once you're at that stage in developing your own inbox magazine, suddenly the information in that chapter will be a lot more relevant.

Above all, don't be afraid to make mistakes. Every inbox magazine will offer different challenges because every target audience is different. Think of this book as more of a guide than a cookbook with specific recipes. Sometimes you can follow the instructions in this book exactly, and sometimes you'll have to modify them for your particular market.

Ultimately, your success will come from you, not from this book. Combine this book's information with your own passion for your topic and your creativity, and you can't help but succeed eventually. Success may look exactly like you dreamed it might be, or it might appear in ways that you never dreamed could have been possible.

Success can be yours as long as you keep learning, keep overcoming obstacles, and keep working toward your ultimate dream. Whatever goals you set for yourself, I know you can achieve them. Now it's up to you to turn your dreams into reality and live the life you've always imagined could be yours one day.

Don't give up and don't let fear stop you from pursuing your dream. Success is closer than you think.

About the Author

MaryEllen Tribby is not your conventional entrepreneur. She was a theater major in college and never took a single business or marketing class.

She credits her long list of accomplishments to the fact that she is able to "marry" her proprietary "love and logic" formula. She has the uncanny ability to take projects that she is passionate about and turn them into profitable ventures over and over again.

Today, MaryEllen Tribby is the premiere business consultant and coach to some of today's most successful entrepreneurs in the information publishing and digital marketing arena. She also works with a number of the largest, most lucrative traditional corporate publishing organizations in the world.

Her quarter century experience includes but is not limited to successfully running multimillion-dollar divisions of companies such as Forbes, Crain's New York Business, and Times Mirror Magazines, later taking the entrepreneurial world by storm as publisher and CEO of Early to Rise, where she was responsible for growing the business from $8 million in sales to $26 million in just 15 months.

Before that, she served as president of Weiss Research, where she led the company to $67 million in sales from $11 million in just 12 months.

In 2008 she founded and remains the proud CEO of **WorkingMomsOnly.com**, the world's leading media company for the empowerment of the working mom.

Her newest venture, **The CEO's Edge** (found at MaryEllen Tribby.com), was born out of necessity. With thousands of entrepreneurs asking for her guidance growing their businesses, she needed to figure out a way to help as many of them as possible. **The CEO's Edge** is the answer!

MaryEllen has transformed the role of CEO with her consulting business. With her multiphase approach, she is able to dissect struggling companies and reengineer them into profitable, respectable organizations. Her belief is in building a solid foundation that will ensure long-term success.

She is known for her "tough love" approach, stating that business is never about revenues—it's always about profits.

One of her international consulting clients recently stated that there are only four or five people in the world that have the diverse level of experience that MaryEllen brings to the table and that she is a clearly a game changer.

MaryEllen is also a highly sought after speaker and author. Her first book, *Changing the Channel: 12 Easy Ways to Make Millions for Your Business*, which she co-authored with Michael Masterson, hit number one on Amazon within just 10 hours of its release.

MaryEllen currently resides in Boca Raton, Florida, with her husband of 17 years, Patrick, and their three beautiful children, Mikaela, Connor, and Delanie, as well as their crazy boxer, Coco.

She sits on the board of several industry associations and has been honored with numerous awards for her excellence in the field of direct response marketing, multichannel marketing, business, and entrepreneurship.

To find out more about MaryEllen, please visit **MaryEllenTribby .com**, and to see a special presentation from MaryEllen, visit **ReinventingtheEntrepreneurBook.com**.

Index

10/13